Henry Cabot Lodge

Historical and political Essays

Henry Cabot Lodge

Historical and political Essays

ISBN/EAN: 9783337076108

Printed in Europe, USA, Canada, Australia, Japan

Cover: Foto ©ninafisch / pixelio.de

More available books at **www.hansebooks.com**

HISTORICAL AND POLITICAL ESSAYS

BY

HENRY CABOT LODGE

BOSTON AND NEW YORK
HOUGHTON, MIFFLIN AND COMPANY
The Riverside Press, Cambridge
1892

TO

FRANCIS PARKMAN

IN TOKEN OF ADMIRATION FOR HIS GREAT WORK

AS AN AMERICAN HISTORIAN, AND FOR

HIS CHARACTER AS A MAN

I MERELY desire, by way of preface, to thank most heartily the publishers of The Atlantic Monthly and Andover Review; my friend, Mr. R. W. Gilder, Editor of The Century; Mr. James Knowles, Editor of The Nineteenth Century; and The New York Tribune, for their kindness in permitting me to reprint the essays which I have brought together here.

H. C. L.

CONTENTS.

HISTORICAL AND POLITICAL ESSAYS

WILLIAM H. SEWARD.[1]

GREAT social and political movements which end either in peaceful or in violent revolution develop two wholly distinct sets of leaders. First come the agitators and fanatics, crying in the wilderness, and cursing alike the actual oppressors, and the Gallios, who "care for none of those things." By their appeals and their invective, by their sufferings and their martyrdom, these early pioneers, if their cause be just, sooner or later arouse the slumbering conscience of the world about them; and when this is thoroughly accomplished their work is really done. The great task then passes to other hands; for although the true fanatic may be able to call the people from their

[1] The *Life of Seward* by his son has appeared since the first publication of this essay in *The Atlantic Monthly* for May, 1884. That extensive and elaborate biography has of course added greatly to our knowledge of the details of Mr. Seward's career, but as it has not altered the view of his character and services which I took in 1884, at the time of the publication of Seward's Works, I have allowed the essay to stand as it was originally written.

tents, he cannot organize them. He is, as a rule, incapable of leadership, or, in other words, of dealing with his fellow-men. He would not be what he is if this were not so; for men of that type must be, in the nature of things, different from the mass of their fellow-beings. They must have the solitary temperament in some form or other, for they are obliged to endure mental and moral, if not social, isolation; they must be imbued with the spirit of the mediæval ascetic, utterly given over to one idea, emotional and unreasonable. Such men have played great parts at all epochs, and are no doubt essential to the progress of the human race. In modern times, however, all important reforms are carried by organization and combination; and this is precisely what extreme and violent agitators, who appear as the precursors of great moral movements, are unable to compass.

Yet although the forces are marshaled and the battle won by others, the extremists who first raised their voices against vested abuses frequently have a compensation in the fact that if they live for some years after the triumph of their cause they are often regarded not only as the champions of a once despised but now successful principle, but also as the men who bore that principle to victory. Mankind love the striking and picturesque, and when they see among them some one who in earlier days sustained a great cause in the midst of persecution and obloquy, and who now rests from his labors with all the world on his side, they are dazzled by the contrast. Not content with awarding him the praise which is rightfully his, they give him credit for much that he did not do, and for achievements wholly alien to men of his type. Time, which sets all things even, remedies this injustice. In history the agitator finds his proper place; and while he obtains the commendation which he really deserves, he is no longer burdened with praise which injures because it is misplaced and inappropriate.

In our anti-slavery struggle, leaders of the two very different classes to which allusion has just been made were of course developed, and I have been led to make the preceding remarks about them because there has been of late a disposition to treat the original and extreme abolitionists as if they not only began the great movement, and carried the conflict for freedom to a successful termination, but as if they were in fact the chief, if not the sole persons concerned. The early and radical abolitionists deserve, and will always receive, honor for their sacrifices, their courage, and their success in awakening the sleeping conscience of the country. This they did, and they are entitled to full credit for this part of the great work. No one would think of denying their heroism in support of a noble principle, or the value of their services to the cause of humanity. At the same time, they are not, except in this indirect way, as the original and exciting cause, the men who actually stopped the extension of slavery, saved the Union, and destroyed human bondage in the United States. To meet and overcome the slave power it was

necessary to form a great political organization,
or, in other words, to obtain the concerted action
of large bodies of men. This the abolitionists
could not do. They did not even have coherence
among themselves. Some of them acted politically; others refused even to vote. Some of them
wished to push the cause of women's rights; others
thought one issue at a time enough. Some favored
a choice between the two great parties; others
would vote for no candidates except their own.
They were continually extending and strengthening
the anti-slavery sentiment among the people, but
they could not add to their own numbers. The
avowal by many of them of secession principles,
coupled with wild denunciation of the constitution,
shocked thousands who deeply sympathized with
their objects, and they were unable to formulate a
practicable plan of action which was capable of
obtaining substantial support. There were of
course all shades of opinion among the abolitionists, and no general description can possibly be
just to each individual. There can be no doubt,
however, that while as a body they powerfully affected public opinion, they were unable to convert
their principles into effective political questions,
and thence into legislative acts.

In one division, the political abolitionists, we find
the germs of a party which, after various modifica-
tions and transformations, developed into the Free-
Soil party, which was constitutional, practical, and
therefore possible; but which, in becoming so, separated from the uncompromising abolitionists of

the most extreme and well-marked type. The work of the new party was to point out and define a ground to which anti-slavery men who had clung to the Whig and Democratic parties could come, and where they could unite for concerted action. This the Free Soilers accomplished; and so well did they succeed that when the crash came and political bonds were loosened a place was provided where all anti-slavery men could gather. From less than two hundred thousand votes in 1852 the constitutional anti-slavery party rose to over a million and a quarter in 1856. This quick and mighty increase could not have come by purely natural processes of growth during four years. It was due chiefly to the sudden concentration of all the opponents of slavery. Public opinion, aroused and formed by the abolition propaganda, was, it is true, terribly stimulated in those four years by the aggressions of the slave power, but the main elements had been developing for a much longer period. When the inevitable operation of the slave question had shattered the Whigs and divided the Democrats, great bodies of men who had been for years in real sympathy, but who had been working with different methods and in different directions, were at last set free. They needed only a rallying point, and that the Free Soilers offered them in the policy of resistance to the extension of slavery in the Territories. When they came together and polled their votes, they were themselves startled at the magnitude of the powerful organization which almost seemed to have sprung into existence in the

night. Now for the first time were the enemies of
slavery united. They came from all sides, — Abolitionists, Free Soilers, Democrats, and Whigs. The
waiting had been long, but they met at length
under one roof and on one platform, the only anti-
slavery men who held aloof being the little band
of non-political abolitionists. In this way the Republican party was formed, but the largest addition
to its strength was composed of Whigs, who came
in under the leadership of the distinguished statesman whose name stands at the head of this essay.

The advent of Seward marked the period when
resistance to slavery ceased to be mere agitation or
the object of isolated efforts, and became a political question, capable of solution by ordinary and
constitutional methods, and the watchword of a
compact and organized party. Seward represented
fully the class of statesmen, who, taking up a great
reform, are able by their wisdom, moderation,
firmness, and above all by their capacity for combination, to secure a large popular following, and
thus carry their principles to victory. These new
leaders were men of great ability and vigorous
character. Some came, like Hale and Julian, from
the old Liberty party ; others, like Adams, Sumner, and Wilson, had been engaged in the Free-
Soil movement ; but most of them were fresh from
their affiliations with the Whig and Democratic
parties, which they now left forever. Coming
from every political quarter and from every part of
the free North, the Republican chiefs were all imbued with a common purpose. They had taken upon

themselves a heavy burden, and if they had known that in addition to the conflict with slavery they were soon to be brought face to face with civil war, and charged with the salvation of the Union, their courage might not have been so cheerful as it was when they faced the country with Frémont and Dayton as their candidates.

To the younger generations in the United States no period is so vague and unfamiliar as that which extends from the compromises of 1850 to the first election of Grant. It is neither contemporary nor historical, and those who cannot remember it have as yet but meagre opportunities of understanding the course of events during those momentous years. The time has come, however, when it is most important that just ideas should prevail in regard to the men who confronted the slave power in its last desperate struggle for supremacy, first at the ballot-box, and then on the battle-field. There ought to be no misapprehension in regard to these men. Their characters, abilities, and services ought to be fully and thoroughly understood, and for this reason the appearance of Seward's works [1] in a new and handsome edition, now extended to five volumes, and covering the years of the war, ought to be generally welcomed and widely read. Nowhere else can we obtain an equally just idea of the purposes and principles of the men who put the anti-slavery movement into such a shape as

[1] *The Works of William H. Seward.* Edited by George E. Baker. In five volumes. New edition. Boston : Houghton, Mifflin & Co. 1884.

to assure practical success, and then performed the
far greater work of saving the Union and carrying
the civil war to a triumphant conclusion. This
could not be said of the writings of many party
leaders ; but Seward was so temperate, so reasonable, so lucid, and at the same time held such a
commanding position before the country from 1850
to 1861, that his speeches must be regarded as the
best authority for the wishes and intentions of the
masses of the Republican party at that period.
Any one ought to be well satisfied to let the case
of the North and of freedom go to the tribunal
of history on Seward's presentation ; and there is
nothing which shows more clearly the absolute
criminality of the slave-ridden South in plunging
the country into war than the fair, vigorous, and
courteous exposition of anti-slavery principles and
purposes which was made by the New York Senator.

By a fortunate coincidence the life of Thurlow
Weed, Seward's closest friend, also comes to the
public at this time.[1] I intend, therefore, with the
aid of this new material and of other authorities as
well, to discuss briefly the career and character of
the man who led the anti-slavery movement from
1850 to 1860, and who afterwards held the seals of
state during the direst perils which have ever beset
us as a people.

William Henry Seward was born in Orange
County, New York, in May, 1801. His father was
a man of education, and apparently not without

---

[1] *Memoir of Thurlow Weed.* By his grandson, Thurlow
Weed Barnes. Boston : Houghton, Mifflin & Co. 1884.

ability. Bred a physician, he not only practiced his profession, but was a farmer, store-keeper, politician, and local magistrate. He was a true Jack-of-all-trades, but was sufficiently master of them to thrive in his various undertakings and amass a considerable fortune, a large part of which he devoted to founding an academy. He was evidently an eccentric man, and very unwise in his mode of bringing up his children. On one occasion he made his son William, when a very little boy, recite a poetical address before some of his neighbors. At the conclusion one of the bystanders asked the child which of his father's somewhat numerous professions he should follow. The boy innocently answered that he intended to be a justice of the peace. Thereupon his father took him severely to task for speaking of an office in the gift of others as if it were the proper subject of a " usurping ambition ; " and this unreasoning severity apparently continued and was habitual.

Seward's evident precocity, joined to early delicacy of health, led to his selection as the member of the family who should receive the highest education then attainable. After the usual school preparation, therefore, he entered Union College, where he was successful in his studies, and popular with both professors and students. Although he was far from being a spendthrift, his father's ill-judged parsimony finally induced the young collegian to run away, and seek his fortune in the South. In Georgia he at once obtained a position as instructor in a newly established academy ; but

before he could enter on his duties he **was discovered,** and summoned home by his parents.   **In this**
excursion he caught his first glimpse of slavery, **to**
which he conceived a strong and instinctive aver-
sion, little dreaming then **that under** his hand and
seal would one day issue the Emancipation Procla-
mation of Abraham Lincoln.

On his return **he went back to college, gradu-
ated in due course, and received his degree.**   His
father's treatment was evidently not forgotten, **and**
it is obvious that there was a marked coolness **be-**
tween them for many years.   Seward's affection in
boyhood and youth was given to his mother, by
whose influence he was brought back from the
South, and whom **he** loved, cherished, and mourned
with an exhibition of feeling quite **unusual** to his
calm nature.   Through his mother he received a
tinge of Irish **blood, to which we may attribute his
easy** temper, sanguine **disposition, and constant**
sympathy with the people **of** that **race.**

On leaving college **Seward** studied **law in the**
city of New **York,** and thence moved **to the little**
village of Auburn, where **he** established **himself,**
married well and most happily, and began the dili-
gent practice of his profession.   With untiring in-
dustry and **a** remarkable capacity **for** hard work,
he soon gathered clients, and his fortunes rose with
those of the little town in which he had made his
home.   The country lawyer was an important **man**
in those days, **and Seward was** soon drawn into the
current of politics, **for** which he **had a** strong natural **aptitude.   He was deeply** patriotic, and had

already delivered one or two addresses which show much thought and power for so young a man. He had been bred a Republican, as the Democrats were then called, and had been taught to believe that all Federalists were traitors and aristocrats. Yet, as he himself remarks, when he came to choose his side in politics, he allied himself with the opponents of the Democracy, and voted against that party ever after. The fact is that by instinct Seward was one of the men who became the political heirs of the Federalists, and no amount of education or artificial prejudice could alter his nature. In theory he was one of the " regular " Democrats, or, in the slang of that day, the " Bucktails ; " but as soon as he entered active politics he went into open opposition to his supposed party. Western New York was deeply interested in canals, and the policy of building these great water-ways strongly appealed to Seward's far-seeing mind. This feeling, strengthened by the friendship then formed with Thurlow Weed, led him into the opposition, which then was composed of a portion of the Democrats and of those voters who had once been Federalists. In this way the would-be Democrat found himself speaking, writing, and voting in behalf of DeWitt Clinton, the champion of internal improvements, whom he had always distrusted, for Governor, and of John Quincy Adams, the opponent of the Virginian dynasty, for President. The action was characteristic of the man. He chose his side deliberately, and on broad public grounds, at an age when prejudice and impulse are far more apt to rule than a cool consideration **of** general principles.

Once engaged, however, he never let go **his** hold, although there were intervals subsequently when he persuaded himself that his public career **was over.   It was of course** impossible that **this should be the case, for he could not** have lived **without political action.   Natural genius and ca-**pacity **are the strongest** agents **in shaping a man's** destiny, and **this was** especially **true of Seward.** In 1833 **he wrote :** " Enthusiasm for the right and ambition for personal distinction are passions of which I cannot divest myself ; and while every day's experience is teaching me that the former is the very agent which must defeat the latter, I am **far** from believing **that** I should be **more** happy **were** I **to** withdraw **altogether from** political ac-**tion."   This** correct **bit of** introspection **was** true when **it was written, and equally true of** all periods of Seward's **life,** from **the** beginning to the end.

When he **had once fairly** started he **moved for-**ward rapidly, **for ability, pleasant** manners, inge-nuity and facility stamped him as a leader.   His first political success **came to him in a** curious **way,** through that oddest of **all** political move-ments, anti-masonry.   **Even** when they **were** old **men,** writing their autobiographies, after the close **of most active careers,** both Seward and Weed **were unable to rid** themselves of **the** idea that there **was real meaning** and force in the anti-ma-sonic agitation.   Beginning as **a local** excitement, induced by **the** folly **and** violence **of a few** headstrong and determined men, anti-masonry developed into a political crusade against secret societies. So far as we can judge now, the only peculiar principle of the anti-masons was to exclude masons from office. In other respects, their creed was that of the National Republicans, or Whigs. They succeeded sufficiently to carry one State in a presidential election, and cast a considerable vote at various times in other States. They crippled the Whigs, then in their infancy, they enlisted the support of such men as John Quincy Adams and William Wirt, and they elected here and there a number of local candidates. It is a matter of profound surprise that they should have accomplished even as much as this, or that they should have contrived to exist for several years. One cannot help suspecting that Weed saw in the violent local feeling about Morgan's abduction an opportunity for a movement which should break the dominant party in the State, and that almost any issue, if once fairly started, would spread and flourish, in the absence of broader questions. There is no evidence that prior to the Morgan case the masons, as such, took part in politics ; and it is inconceivable that intelligent men and shrewd politicians should have supposed that any party could really endure, when it had no principle except opposition to secret societies, which were perfectly legal and proper, beneficial to their members, and wholly harmless to every one else. In western New York, the scene of Morgan's abduction, the anti-masonic feeling was of course most intense, and there, at least, the anti-masons effected one excellent result by taking up Seward, who had thrown himself into the movement with great vigor, and sending him to the state senate for two successive terms, placing him in this way in the line of political advancement.

In the condition of politics at that time, when everything was in a state of solution, it mattered comparatively little whether the anti-masons were a sound party or not, provided that they opened the way for young and energetic men to enter politics. Seward owed them much for giving him his opportunity, which is all any man can demand of fate, and he certainly made the most of his, for he had this great quality of success strongly developed.

It is amusing to read his own account of his first speech at Albany, which he delivered in a condition of blind confusion, and to reflect that this embarrassed orator was the man who, in the Senate of the United States, faced for ten years a desperate and fierce majority of slaveholders, and argued with unsurpassed clearness and courage the cause of freedom. After the ice was once broken, however, Seward moved on easily enough. He had a fine gift of speech, and was fortunate also in being, during these first four years, one of a hopeless minority, — the best training which a young man can have for a political and parliamentary career.

The senate of New York was then a highly important body, for, in addition to its legislative functions, it sat as a court of last appeal, after the fashion of the House of Lords. Seward thus had an opportunity to establish his legal as well as his parliamentary reputation. How well he succeeded is shown by the fact that his skillful and bold resistance to the measures of the all-powerful Jacksonian Democracy and his ability in dealing with all local questions made him at the close of his second term, and when he was only thirty-three years old, the acknowledged leader of the opposition in the State. This was so universally admitted that in 1834 he was put forward as the candidate of the young Whig party for governor, and, although defeated, made a fine run and polled a large vote.

Thus thrown out of the race, Seward returned to the law, avowing that his political career was ended, and resolved on professional success. His business rapidly revived, but the abstention from politics, which was to have been absolute, was in reality so purely imaginary that in 1838 he was again nominated for governor by the Whigs, then just on the eve of their first great success. This time he was triumphantly elected, and on the 1st of January, 1839, before he had attained his thirty-ninth year, was duly inaugurated at Albany.

Space forbids that I should trace in detail the busy years of Seward's governorship, except in so far as he was concerned with the great question to which his life was to be devoted. He made an admirable governor, and in regard to all issues of the day, on internal improvements, education, prison reform, and other less important matters, he exhibited the breadth of view, the foresight, and the courage of opinion which were his most conspicuous qualities as a statesman. Seward was naturally prudent and cautious; he was always regarded as a keen and wary politician, and in his later career his enemies charged that he was given to cunning and time-serving. Yet if any one now dispassionately studies his course as governor, the most marked characteristics of the man, and those which, if we take the pains to understand him, were never, either then or afterwards, lost or impaired, were his entire courage and complete superiority to clamor and prejudice. This was shown by his fearless independence of party and popular feeling on many state questions, and especially by his liberality toward Roman Catholics. His course on various matters, deliberately adopted in opposition to the views of his more careful friends, caused him to fall several thousand votes behind the ticket when he was reëlected; but he neither heeded warnings when they were uttered, nor grieved over their subsequent fulfillment, because he was satisfied that he was right. In nothing was his independence better shown than in the constantly recurring questions of pardons. The rich, prosperous, strong, and well educated, who had fallen into crime, and came with powerful and influential support in search of mercy, were sent to prison or to the gallows, to meet their merited punishment. The poor, unfortunate, and neglected were those who received executive clemency, which was exercised with kindly wisdom, and at the same time with a moderation which is in strong contrast to the indiscriminate use of the pardoning power now so unfortunately common.

There was one question, however, then just beginning to cast its ominous shadow over the land, which dwarfed all others, and brought to a crucial test the mental and moral strength of the young governor of New York. It was, in fact, at this time that Seward was first brought into actual conflict with the slave power. Before the election the New York abolitionists addressed a series of questions to both the Whig and the Democratic candidates for governor and lieutenant-governor. The latter, avowed pro-slavery men, treated these inquiries with silent contempt; the former returned respectful answers. Seward's response shows a little of the adroitness which was popularly attributed to him. He contrived to manifest his entire sympathy with the opposition to slavery, but he declined, properly enough, to make ante-election pledges, and left his position to be guessed at rather than known. It was the only utterance of his life on that great question which any one could think of calling evasive, and his acts quickly showed that his prudence had no touch of timidity. Very soon after his election he was called upon by the governor of Virginia to surrender three negro sailors, accused of helping a slave, who had been since recaptured, to escape from servitude. Seward declared that the evidence on which the demand was based was wholly insufficient, and not content with this took up the broad ground that New York did not recognize assistance to a fugitive slave to be a crime, and therefore he could not comply with the requisition. He said to the governor of Virginia,

" I need not inform you, sir, that there **is no law of**
this State which recognizes slavery, — no statute
which admits that one man can be the property of
another, or that one man can be stolen from an-
other. On the other hand, our constitution and
laws interdict slavery in every form. Nor is **it**
necessary to inform you that the common law does
not recognize slavery, nor make the act of which
the parties **are accused in this case** felonious or
criminal. The offense **charged in the** affidavit,
and specified in the requisition, **is not a felony nor**
a crime within the meaning of the constitution,
and, waiving all the defects in the affidavit, I cannot surrender the supposed fugitives, to be carried
to Virginia for trial under the statute of that
State." These were bold words, and we can hardly
realize the shock they produced in that day, when
Northern office-holders were wont to hasten, with
bated breath, to do the bidding of the South. Such
language **people** expected from abolition fanatics ;
but coming **from a** man who held a high and responsible office, it had a startling effect. The enemies of slavery took heart, and **it was** evident to all
who looked beyond the immediate present that **a**
new leader had appeared in American politics.

Through the long controversy which ensued Sew-
ard never abated by one tittle the high, firm, and
yet courteous tone which **he** had adopted at the
outset. **He remained** unmoved by the retaliatory
measures of Virginia, which threatened to prevent
the surrender of ordinary criminals escaping from
New York. He also defended the New York law,

then a subject of much irritation at the South, which gave to fugitive slaves the right of trial by jury. He refused to comply with a requisition from South Carolina, similar to that made by Virginia; and when, in his second term, a Democratic assembly undertook to disapprove his action, he declined to transmit their resolutions to the Virginian authorities. At the close of his second term he voluntarily retired from office, and renewed the practice of his profession; but his conduct in regard to fugitive slaves had sunk deep into the public mind. He probably did not realize it himself, but the calm, high courage which, as governor, he had displayed on this question had marked him out as the future leader of the anti-slavery movement. It was now inevitable that when the time came men would turn to him, and put him at their head as the chosen captain in the warfare which was to check the extension of slavery through the virgin Territories and the free States of the North.

When Seward left Albany in January, 1843, the first period of his life closed, and he himself felt that his career as a public man was at an end. He had received the highest honor within the gift of the people of his State, and was content. But the real work of his life was still to be done, and the time was to come when he would be called forth by that imperious public necessity which at the appointed hour surely brings the man. Before that hour came, there was a long interval of six years, which he devoted to his profession, and during which he made his fame as a lawyer. Seward pos-

sessed legal abilities of a very high **order, and his**
time was constantly occupied with arguments before the Supreme Court of the United States and
the highest state tribunals.   The most extensive
and lucrative part of his **profession** was in patent
cases, an intricate branch which he took up com-
paratively late in life, and in which he speedily **be-**
came proficient by his quick, clear perceptions, his
versatility of mind, and his unfailing industry.

It was as a jury lawyer, however, that Seward touched his highest point professionally, and
achieved a reputation which **very** few advocates
have equaled.   Some of the cases, notably the defense of Greeley in Cooper's libel suit, and of the
Michigan rioters, made a great stir in their day,
although they **are now** well-nigh forgotten.   His
arguments before the Supreme Court of the United
States in two famous fugitive-slave cases, although
not addresses to a jury, had some of the popular
qualities **belonging** to the latter, **and by their** fearless **ability attracted widespread** attention.   There
is one **case,** however, in **which** Seward was engaged
at this period **that** cannot be passed **over with a**
mere allusion ; for there is scarcely any event in **his**
life which displays **his** highest and strongest quali-
ties in a better light.

In 1846 Seward had voluntarily acted as counsel
for a convict named Wyatt, who had murdered one
of his keepers, and he had rested the defense on
the ground **of insanity.**   There **was a** good deal of
feeling about **the case, and** when the jury disagreed
Seward came in for much animadversion.   Before

Wyatt could be brought again to trial a whole family, respectable and prosperous people, were butchered at Auburn by a negro named Freeman, recently discharged from the state prison. The popular excitement was intense. Freeman narrowly escaped lynching, and the universal rage at his atrocious crime reached even to the bench. So strong, indeed, was the feeling that it was generally believed that no one could be found who would dare to act as counsel for the murderer. Seward was satisfied of what was unquestionably the truth, — that the wretched criminal was not only demented, but so hopelessly idiotic as to be little removed from the brutes. A jury was summoned to pass upon Freeman's sanity, and when the court asked who appeared for the prisoner Seward rose, and undertook the defense. The jury decided in substance that Freeman was sane enough to be hanged, and he was at once put on trial. The miserable wretch, deaf and idiotic, could not even plead guilty or not guilty, and when asked who was his counsel replied that he did not know. Then Seward rose again, pale with excitement, but cool and determined, and announced that he would act as counsel. Hoarse murmurs of indignation ran through the crowded court-room. Friends and neighbors turned their backs on the daring lawyer, and there was hardly anybody who would speak to him. With perfect courage, however, Seward conducted the case to the end, using every fair means of defense; but wholly in vain, for Freeman was in reality condemned before he was tried. After the sentence Seward appealed to the governor, but pardon was refused. He then moved the Supreme Court for a new trial, which was granted; but before it came on Freeman died in jail, and the post-mortem examination revealed a brain diseased to the last point.

Seward's action in taking this case showed not only humanity and generosity of the finest type, but courage of an uncommon quality. It was no light matter to face, alone and unsupported, the fierce prejudice and intense excitement of the community in which he lived, in behalf of a low, brutalized criminal, belonging to a despised and hated race. There was no hope or prospect of reward of any kind. There was nothing to tempt any man in such a revolting task. Seward took up the ungracious work with nothing before him at the moment as a result but universal hatred and condemnation; and he made this sacrifice solely from devotion to the principles of law and justice in which he had been bred. Not content, moreover, with doing his simple duty as counsel, he appealed to the jury in a speech of impassioned fervor and consummate ability. There are very few jury speeches which can be ranked above it, and that this statement is not an exaggeration is proved by the opinion of the greatest of modern English orators. Mr. Gladstone said to Mr. Sumner, "Mr. Seward's argument in the Freeman case is the greatest forensic effort in the English language." An English gentleman who was present said, "The greatest? Mr. Gladstone, you forget Erskine."

"No," replied Mr. Gladstone, "I do not forget Erskine; Mr. Seward's argument is the greatest forensic effort in the language." With such praise from such a judge we may be content to leave the question of Seward's powers as a jury lawyer and forensic orator.

Although Seward, during these years of devotion to the law, believed that he had permanently withdrawn to private and professional life, he found it impossible, after having held the office of governor and been an acknowledged leader of public opinion, to keep entirely aloof from politics. His aid and direction were constantly sought, and he could not, consistently with his views of public duty, refuse to give them. He supported Clay in 1844, Taylor in 1848, and Scott in 1852. During this time his hostility to slavery strengthened and deepened from day to day, and he became more and more outspoken on that burning question. His well-known views on slavery, indeed, led to the unfounded charge that his support of Clay was insincere and half-hearted. No accusation was ever more untrue, but it arose from Seward's public, explicit, and repeated expressions of regret that the brilliant Whig candidate should be a slave-holder. With even greater heartiness, but still with the same reservation, he supported Taylor; and again, after his return to public life, advocated the election of Scott, despite the approval given to the pro-slavery compromises by the Whig platform. If Seward had been a timid shuffler, such a course would not have been surprising; but since he **was so** pronounced **and** hardy an opponent of slavery that he even received the encomium of Wendell Phillips, it seems at first sight somewhat inexplicable.   **We** can in fact understand **his action only by a** perfect comprehension **of his views in regard to parties, and as to the most advantageous manner in which any** man **could aid the progress of the principles he had most at heart.   The subject is well worth study,** especially by those who **seek to promote some** important reform ; because in this way can be learned the philosophy of a man who by well-judged action did as much for the advancement of a great cause **as** any man of equal talent who has ever lived **among us,** and **who,** wasting nothing, made himself **count to the** uttermost.

When a very young man, Seward says, he came to the conclusion that, "whatever might be a man's personal **convictions, and however** earnestly he might desire **to promote the** public welfare, he could only **do it** by associating himself with one of the many religious sects which divided **the community, and one of the two** political parties which contended **for the** administration **of** the **government.   A** choice between sects **and** parties **once** made, whether wisely or unwisely, **it** was easy to **see,** must **be** practically irrevocable. . . . But **though I thus** chose my religious denomination and political **party, I did** so with **a** reservation **of a** right **to** dissent **and** protest, or even separate, **if** ever **a** conscientious sense of duty **or** a paramount **regard to** the general safety or welfare should re-

quire." In 1844 a young friend, of strong abolition principles, consulted him about leaving his
church and party because of their weakness in respect to slavery. Seward said, "If you had the
power, would you regard it as wise to abstract from
the Presbyterian church of this country all its anti-
slavery element, or would you desire to add to it
all the anti-slavery reinforcement you could command? How much better off would that church
be with all you anti-slavery men out of it? How
much better off, to do any good, would you be if
all withdrew? Would you thereby gain any more
personal influence than you now have? Look at
the Whig party of to-day. Everybody knows that
I am an anti-slavery man. Whenever I write a
political letter, or make a political speech, my
words are reproduced in every Whig paper in the
country, and reach the eyes and ears of everybody
in the land. But it is because I remain in the
party, and consequently enjoy their confidence.
They will hear me and consider what I say. But
should I leave the Whig party, and join the radical anti-slavery party, although my speeches and
writings would doubtless be read by that class who
do not need my influence, they would not reach the
much larger class who do need to know the truth.
No; I think I can do more good where I am. . . .
Stick to the ship, and work away. In a few years
you will see that we anti-slavery men in the Whig
party will not have labored in vain. Do you be as
faithful in your church as I will try to be in the
Whig party, and you will see that, if you would do

your fellow-men any good at all, you must **not**
withdraw yourself from **their** association because
you think you know more or are better than they
are."

In **1848 he spoke at Cleveland,** where there
was **great danger of a serious defection** of anti-
slavery **Whigs.** In the course of his speech, which
was **most eloquent and effective, he said,** " You
expect **to establish a new and better party,** that
will **carry our common principles to more speedy**
and universal triumph. **You will not succeed in**
any degree, either now **or** hereafter, because **it is**
impossible. Society is divided, classified, already.
It is classified into two great, all-pervading national parties or associations. **These** parties are
founded on the principles, interests, and affections
of the people. **Society cannot admit, nor** will it
surrender either of the existing parties to make
room **for, a third. The interests, the sentiments,**
and **the habits of society forbid : —**

> " ' The stars in their courses war against Sisera.'

It is in the power of a seceding **portion of one**
party, or of seceding portions **of** both, to **do just**
this, and no **more, to wit :** to give success, long **or**
short, to one of the existing parties. Those who
do this, whatever be their objects **or motives, are**
responsible **for the** consequences. Theirs is the
merit if the consequences are beneficent, and theirs
is the blame if the result is calamitous." Seven
years later a new party was founded, and Seward
made one of his greatest political speeches at Al-

bany on " The Advent of the Republican Party."
A few brief extracts show his line of thought:
" You, old, tried, familiar friends, ask my counsel
whether to cling yet longer to traditional contro-
versies and to dissolving parties, or to rise at once
to nobler aims, with new and more energetic associations. I do not wonder at your suspense, nor
do I censure caution or even timidity. Fickleness
in political associations is a weakness, and precipi-
tancy in public action is a crime. Considered by
itself, it is unfortunate to be obliged to separate
from an old party and to institute a new one."
Then, in discussing the question whether the time
for a new party had arisen, he made that famous
exposition of the " privileged classes," or slave
power, which rang from one end of the country
to the other; and when he came to the end of his
description he asked, " What, then, is wanted ?
Organization! Organization! Nothing but organization! Shall we organize ?, Why not ? Can we
maintain the revolution so auspiciously begun without organization? Certainly not. . . . *How* shall
we organize? The evil is a national one. The
power and the influence and the organization of
the privileged class pervade all parts of the Union.
Our organization, therefore, must be a national
one." After depicting the character of the organization required, he said, " It is best to take an
existing organization that answers to these conditions, if we can find one; if we cannot find one
such, we must create one. Let us try existing
parties by this test. . . . Shall we report our-

selves to the Whig party? Where is it? Gentle
shepherd, tell me where! . . . The privileged class,
who had debauched it, abandoned it because they
knew that it could not vie with its rival in the
humiliating service it proffered them; and now
there is neither Whig party nor Whig south
of the Potomac. How is it in the unprivileged
States? Out of New York the lovers of freedom,
disgusted with its prostitution, forsook it, and
marched into any and every other organization.
We have maintained it here, and in its purity,
until the aiders and abettors of the privileged class,
in retaliation, have wounded it on all sides, and it
is now manifestly no longer able to maintain and
carry forward, alone and unaided, the great revolution that it inaugurated. He is unfit for a statesman, although he may be a patriot, who will cling
even to an honored and faithful association when
it is reduced so low in strength and numbers as to
be entirely ineffectual, amid the contests of great
parties by which republics are saved. Any party,
when reduced so low, must ultimately dwindle and
dwarf into a mere faction. Let, then, the Whig
party pass."

It must not be forgotten, in considering Seward's
utterances on these matters, that he was as far removed as possible from being a thick-and-thin partisan. I doubt if any man of modern times has left
a collection of political speeches, delivered for the
most part at a period of intense excitement, which
are so absolutely free from undue partisanship;
for Seward rarely discussed men, but confined him-

self to measures and principles, and he never appealed to mere party allegiance for votes. He was
not a partisan, but he was a strong believer in
parties, because he thought that only through parties any practical and beneficent result could be
achieved. History and experience taught him that
in representative governments there could be at
once only two great parties having any effective
life. A third party, while the two leading parties
held their strength, was simply a faction, and the
multiplication of parties was the multiplication of
factions, with all the evils incident to political
anarchy. His primary test of a party was its
capacity for efficient work, and this was to be
largely determined by its numbers and the vigor
of its organization. He also well understood that
a third party could have but one result, — the
defeat of the organization to which it was most
nearly allied in character and purpose. For this
reason he opposed third-party movements, and he
maintained his party standing because he deemed
it the most efficient weapon he possessed for the
successful advancement of a cause which he placed
above party. From such motives he refused to
leave the Whigs, although he held quite as radical
views about slavery as the Free Soilers in 1848
and 1852. Thanks to his sanguine temperament,
he continued to hope that the Whigs could be
made the party of freedom; but when that party
perished, not in the least through the third-party
action, but by the operation of the slavery question and by its own inherent vices, no one recog-

nized its dissolution more quickly **than Seward.**
In 1855 the time **had** come for him to move,
and then **was seen** the **force** of his position.   He
marched not alone, but with thousands at his back,
and wielding greater influence than ever, to join
the ranks **of** the **Republicans,** who sprang at once
to **the front,** not **as a third or fourth** faction, but
as one of the two great political divisions of the
country.   **In this way the overthrow of slavery**
was made certain, and in **no other manner could it**
have been brought about.

Seward's course teaches the wholesome lesson
that men may work in thorough sincerity for the
same end, although in very different ways ; and
that attacks on parties, under our system, simply
because they **are organizations, is idle** nonsense.
There is no necessary or peculiar virtue in remain-
ing **outside of parties, or in belonging to third
parties or** small **factions, although** they may be
important **and useful factors in solving political**
problems.   **There is no greater mistake or more**
illiberal habit than to assail **men for belonging to**
parties.   **No** greater injury can **be done to any**
cause than **by** belittling a **leader who,** earnestly
favoring **it, has at the** same time **party** standing
and influence, or by persuading **such a** man to cast
away that which increases his value and effect
enormously, and to come out of his organization
while **it is still powerful,** and reduce himself **to**
mere isolated **action.**   Seward would have been a
leader, **and a great one,** whatever position he might
have chosen to occupy ; but by his wise course he

counted a hundred-fold more for the cause of human freedom than he could have done in any other way.

The wave of Whig success which carried Taylor to the White House made Seward Senator from New York, and the great period of his life began. His influence opened Taylor's eyes to the plain fact that the South was the real aggressor, and that her outcries against Northern interference were merely intended to mislead. When his mind was once made up the old soldier did not hesitate. Although unversed in the ways of politics, he saw clearly that the duty of the hour was to admit California ; and he gave it to be clearly understood that if Congress would perform its part he would do his, and would see to it that the republic was not injured or the Union impaired. This policy Seward advocated with great force in the Senate ; but neither he nor the President could hold their own party. The Whigs gave way in all directions, and their fate was sealed. Seward had hoped that the Whigs might become the party of freedom ; and if they had followed his lead and Taylor's in 1850, they might have done the work and reaped the glories and the reward of the Republicans. They failed at the supreme moment, and thus went down into the dust ; for great issues are inexorable, and when they are not obeyed they crush.

From the Whig chiefs themselves came the policy of compromise — or, in other words, of concession — to slavery. Webster fell on the 7th of March, and Seward, with unflinching courage,

stepped into the vacant place, and grasped **the
standard** of the free North as it dropped from **the
hands** of the great Senator from Massachusetts.
He stoutly contested the compromises, but all in
vain. That policy succeeded, **and its** brief victory
cost **the Whig party its life.** There **were a** few
years of **seeming peace,** and then the strife broke
out again. **The South tore the compromises of**
1850 **asunder.** **They seized Kansas by the throat,**
and **kept her** in **anarchy and misery because** she
would not accept slavery, and **thus made it clear**
that only slave States were to be admitted to the
Union. Goaded on by the inherent weakness of
their cause, they next destroyed the Missouri Compromise, and in **so** doing bent even the Supreme
Court to their **purposes.** **At last everything was
theirs.** **They had thrown open the** Territories to
slaves ; they would admit no States but slave
States **; and the next step would have been to force**
slavery **upon the free** States, **and make them, if**
not slave-holders, slave-catchers. But **in winning**
these Pyrrhic **victories they sealed their own ruin,**
and it fell **to** Seward to lead the new **party,** which
Southern madness did so much **to build up.**

The years preceding **the war are so** murky with
the tempests of passion and **hate which** raged
through **them** that it is even now difficult to see
them clearly. **On** that dark background a **few**
figures **stand out luminous** and distinct, — **men**
with **clear** views and perfect courage, and conspicuous among them **is** Seward. **In** his speeches in
the Senate we can trace all the phases of **the**

struggle. We see him beaten on one question after another, and then the tide turns, and he moves forward to success. It is on that period and on the debates of that time that Seward's reputation as a parliamentary orator must rest. There is a very even excellence in these speeches. The Kansas-Nebraska speech of 1854 is very noble and fine, and the careful and cutting attack on Pierce in 1856 is extremely effective; but selection is difficult and unfair, for the whole series deserves high rank. Seward was not eloquent after the manner of Webster and Clay. He lacked the grandeur as well as the dramatic force and sweep of the former, and the impassioned fervor so marked in the latter. His speeches, however, have outlived those of Clay, and will always be read with pleasure and interest both for their subjects and their style. Their most striking trait is the blending of grace and strength, which is a very rare combination. Graceful speakers as a rule have little force, and are the most ephemeral of orators. But Seward, despite his smoothness and grace, had the root of the matter in him, and all he said went home with telling effect. In his earlier days he had a tendency, which was very common at that time, to indulge in rhetorical outbursts. He did not become turgid at such moments, but he occasionally was guilty of commonplace fine writing. As he grew older his taste improved, and by the time he reached the Senate of the United States he had freed himself entirely from this fault, and his style, although not particularly simple, was pure and

clear.   He had, too, a remarkable power **of strong,
lucid, and** ingenious statement and great variety
in presentation.   **He was** never dull, and yet at
the same time he had **a** reason and moderation in
expression which rendered **all he said** convincing,
and made him especially valuable **to an** unpopular
cause which needed converts.   His speeches did
more than anything else to formulate a creed by
which **all the anti-slavery elements in the country**
could live and work **unitedly.   Seward had also**
considerable felicity **of** quotation ; for although
not a scholar, he read widely and well, and remembered much.   He was gifted likewise with a fine
humor, dry and quizzical, but very attractive and
singularly effective in debate.   This quality comes
out strongly in many passages of his autobiogra-
phy, which is very charming, and has by no means
the reputation that it deserves.

He employed humor discreetly and with much
effect **in his speeches.   In 1853, in a** speech on
Continental **rights** and relations, **he** said, "**Sec-**
ondly, **the** Senator **from Michigan** invokes **our**
attention to what Lord George **Bentinck has said**
in the British Parliament.   Well, sir, that **is im-**
portant, — what an English **lord** has said, and **said
in** Parliament, **too ;** that must **be** looked into.
Well, what did Lord George Bentinck say ?   Sir,
he said very angry things, very furious things ; indeed, **very ferocious** things.   Prepare yourself to
hear **them, sir.   Lord George** Bentinck did say, in
so many words, — **and** in Parliament, too ! — what
I am going to **repeat.   His lordship** did **say that**
— ' he quite **agreed with Captain Polkington.**' "

The whole passage runs on at a length too great for quotation, but in the same vein ; and the Senator from Michigan must have devoutly wished, at the conclusion, that he had never alluded to Lord George Bentinck. Further extracts might be made if space would permit, but those who desire to use fun and irony in debate, without degenerating into buffoonery, cannot do better than study these speeches. They are good models in that way as well as in many others.

After the repeal of the Missouri Compromise there was a short period when even Seward's constitutional cheerfulness gave way ; but he made no sign at the time, and hope soon returned. We can detect the tone of rising confidence in everything he says, as he became convinced that Kansas could not be conquered, and that the spirit of the North was at last aroused.

When 1860 came Thurlow Weed felt that the time had arrived for Seward's candidacy for the presidency, and this feeling was shared by the mass of the party in the strong Republican States, and by the ablest leaders everywhere ; for Seward was their acknowledged chief and their most conspicuous statesman. When the Republican delegates assembled at Chicago there was no man in the country who had such claims and such a reputation, or who was such an exponent of their principles, as the New York Senator. But Seward was now to reap the reward of years of eminence and conflict. There was a strong movement made against him on the ground of availability, and in-

stigated by personal hostility, which **was at first**
laughed at, but which steadily assumed more **for-**
midable proportions. The attack was headed by
Horace Greeley, and Greeley and those who
thought with him prevailed. **The** convention became **convinced that** Seward was **not** available,
and Lincoln was nominated on the third ballot.
When the Republicans **made this choice they**
builded far better than they knew ; for they took
the one **man who had all the elements of greatness,**
and all the qualities which fitted him beyond **any**
one else in the country to stand at the head of a
great nation in the agonies of civil war. By their
selection they also made it possible to unite **Lin-**
coln and Seward **in** the cabinet, — each **in** the
place for which **he was** best adapted. But all this
the Republicans **at** Chicago could not know at the
moment, and their action carried dismay and bitter
regret **not merely to Seward's** immediate **friends,**
but to the masses of the party **in the Eastern States.**
Seward **himself showed** no sign **of** the disappointment he must have **felt.** With perfect and hearty
cheerfulness **he gave his** adhesion **to the** ticket,
and, feeling that **he was still the** responsible leader
of the campaign, **he put himself in** the **forefront**
of the battle. The **entire magnanimity of** Seward's
course shows that with **him devotion to his cause**
was far stronger than any personal ambition.

The speeches which Seward made during **this**
campaign must **be** taken in conjunction with those
which he delivered during **the** campaign **of 1856,**
and **together they form** a complete presentation of

the case of the anti-slavery party. At the outset
he portrayed the manner in which the slave-holding aristocracy had gained entire possession of
every department of the government. He then
delineated the "irrepressible conflict" of freedom
and slavery, and brought home to the North the
conviction that one or the other must perish; that
even the North American continent did not afford
room for their joint existence. He defined the Republican position so that it was plain to all men
that it was constitutional and lawful, and that,
while his party proposed to stop the extension of
slavery, it would not interfere with the guaranteed
rights of the States. Finally, in the Senate he demonstrated the truth of Sumner's proposition, that
" freedom was national, and slavery sectional," by
inviting the Southern Senators to come to the
North and argue their cause before the people, who
there would give them fair hearing and free speech,
while in the South a man who dared to speak in
public against slavery was hunted to death, or
driven from the State. A cause which thus stifled
free speech was in its nature irredeemably vicious
and sectional, and nothing was more effective than
the manner in which Seward drove this fact home.

To Seward's speeches at this time men will always look for the official announcement of Republican principles prior to 1861, and by them it is
proved, if proof is needed, that the cry that the
election of Lincoln meant the destruction of Southern rights and Southern property was the meanest
excuse ever put forward to cover a great political
crime.

According to Seward's argument, the election of
Lincoln meant the stoppage of slave extension,
and that the South would have no choice but to
submit to the popular will, or to go into open revolution. To his sanguine mind and loyal temperament the latter alternative seemed incredible; but
when he returned to Washington, after the election, he found civil war actually at the gates.
Seward believed, and believed correctly, that the
fact of the election of Lincoln really settled the
question of slavery; because when the people said
to slavery, Thus far shalt thou go, and no farther,
the end had come, inasmuch as without extension
slavery must sooner or later perish utterly. With
this belief Seward saw the far greater question of
national existence open before him. The Union
was in danger, and if the Union were to dissolve
it mattered little what became of the slave question, with two confederacies, — one wholly free,
and the other wholly slave-holding, existing side by
side. He therefore pushed the slavery question
aside, and threw his whole energies into the work
of saving the Union. He advocated the cause of
conciliation and peace in a great speech; and
while he did not abate one jot of the true result
of the election, the stoppage of slave extension, he
set it aside for the time being as inferior to the
work of maintaining the Union.

From heated partisans, and from radical men
generally, there went up a cry that Seward had
lost heart, and was about to betray the cause of
freedom; and from this time dates the notion,

assiduously cultivated in hours of great excitement, that he was a timid time-server. Nothing could be more unjust. Seward felt that his first duty, and that of every loyal citizen, was to save the Union; and that the danger from slavery, except as a means of destroying the Union, had passed. He also saw clearly that the government must be held together in some way until the new administration came in. Largely through his efforts treason in Buchanan's cabinet was checked, and together with Stanton and Dix he then labored to keep the peace and strengthen the Federal power. Lincoln, with intuitive wisdom, had selected Seward to abide at his right hand, in the trial that was upon them; and when they at last took the helm they agreed wholly about the course which they ought to steer. Lincoln perceived, without any instruction, that the first thing was to preserve our national existence. So he and his secretary strove to keep the States together by peaceful means, and failed. They struggled next to narrow the limits of the rebellion by holding the border States; but as is always the case when revolution is afoot, the extreme men were at the front on both sides, the strong tide of passion was sweeping all before it, and they failed again. They made one further great effort. They resolved to make the war wholly and distinctly a war for the Union, and not allow it to be placed on any other ground. In this they succeeded, and by so doing they stopped disintegration in the North, broke down party lines, and brought a thoroughly united people to their side, entirely imbued with the determination to maintain the nation. This task of uniting the loyal people of the country was the first and essential step toward victory, and it was peculiarly the work of Lincoln and Seward.

If we study the war purely as history, the most striking fact is the inevitable character of the result, although at the time it appeared as if the outcome hung in grave doubt down to the very end. There was only one moment, if we thus survey that period, when it seems as if the final result might have lost its inevitable character, and that was at the time of the Trent affair. If Lincoln and Seward had wavered and yielded to the popular clamor, and we had rushed into war with England and France, it is doubtful if we could have crushed the South with one hand, and beaten off the two greatest powers of the civilized world with the other. Lincoln, as the head of the administration, was responsible for the action of the government, and with all his good nature and easy ways he was too great a man to be other than master in his cabinet. Still, there can be no doubt that he leaned on Seward in this question. Seward of course wrote the letter, which was entirely right both in law and policy, and it was a production which bore all the characteristics of its author. At the time, fierce passions were aroused ; the people were justly incensed at the attitude of England; and the young men of the country, with arms in their hands, were eager to fight all comers. On Lincoln and Seward fell the responsibility of the action, and history

will record it as one of the wisest and greatest acts
of his and the President's life. But at the moment
it caused an increase of the feeling that Seward
was adroit and timid, and this mere prejudice became so strong that it is only now that Seward is
beginning to receive the place which belongs to
him and the praise which he merits.

The diplomatic diary and correspondence, con-
tained in the fifth volume of the works, are extremely interesting, and enable us to form a just
estimate of their author's great services during the
war. Mr. Lincoln allowed him in large measure
to select his ministers to foreign courts, and this
momentous work was performed with great skill.
The volume throws light only on the general course
of the war and on our relations with foreign nations; but nowhere else do we obtain such striking
evidence of the inevitable character of the result
of our struggle, to which allusion has already been
made. This arises from the fact that Seward took
a comprehensive view of the whole situation. Behind the operation of armies, which he surveyed
on a large scale, he saw the other aspects of the
conflict. He perceived and understood the inherent feebleness of the insurgent States, which was
lost to others in the din of arms and the smoke of
battle. He detected and rightly valued the innate
weaknesses of the Confederacy, arising from the
nature of their cause, the existence of human slavery among them, their lack of resources, the ruin
caused by the blockade, and their financial un-
soundness.

It was well for the Union that Seward was a man able at once to see, appreciate, and express all these things. Our representatives abroad, depressed by the hostile influences about them, by the seeming slowness of our military progress, and by the constant disappointment of their hopes, often lost heart. All their gloomy forebodings were poured out upon the Secretary of State, to whom they confided also all their troubles and anxieties. Nothing, of course, was more essential than that the United States should have a confident and calm demeanor before Europe, and it rested with Seward to see that our ministers did not forget this all-important fact. Fortunately for us, no man could have been chosen who was better prepared, by temperament and by training, for this most trying and difficult task. By nature extremely sanguine, Seward had also a profound confidence in his country and in the American people. His dispatches have a clear ring in them, which must have aroused even the most faint-hearted. Gloom and despair might settle elsewhere, but at no time were they permitted to rest upon the department of State. Seward never boasted unduly, he never sought to disguise defeat, but he always reviewed the whole situation so reasonably, so vigorously, and in such a masterly way that his correspondents caught his spirit, and believed with him that the end could be nothing but victory. No one can question that Seward himself had his dark hours, but his self-control was never lost, and to the European world, looking and longing with scarcely disguised eagerness for the destruction of the republic, he bore himself with a proud and assured confidence, which was of infinite value in that time of stress and doubt.

There is the same tone in all that relates to the perilous and difficult complications with foreign powers produced by the war. At home the disposition was to consider Seward over-cautious. Abroad, the reverse was the case. In reality Seward's policy was both bold and aggressive, and yet was so tempered by prudence that it never degenerated into rashness. He convinced foreign powers of our readiness to fight, which was of inestimable value, and which enabled us better than anything else to keep clear of actual hostilities. This comes out very strongly in the treatment of the Mexican question, and in the determination and tenacity with which the Alabama claims were pressed. There is a great debt of gratitude due to Seward for his wisdom and courage as minister of foreign affairs at the most trying period of our history.

When the war closed Seward sympathized fully with the generous and magnanimous policy which Lincoln marked out in his second inaugural. The death of the President threw the country into the hands of Johnson, and confusion followed. Seward believed that Johnson's intentions were honest, and that he meant to follow the policy of Lincoln; but he also saw plainly the hopeless errors of the President's manner and methods. He thought that Congress, too, made mistakes, and yet purposed well. In short, he perceived that there was good in both the contending parties, but he could not allay the strife. So he contented himself with pushing forward various negotiations which he had much at heart, and referred in a speech at Auburn to the conflict between the President and Congress with the dry humor which had been a good deal eclipsed during the days of battle. The truth was that ordinary partisanship had become impossible to Seward. It died within him when, standing by the side of Lincoln, he had looked down into the seething gulf of civil war and faced the awful thought of a divided empire. The saying of Douglas, "Henceforth there can be only two parties, the party of patriots and the party of traitors," had entered deep into his soul. Like Andrew, "he had stood as a high priest between the horns of the altar, and poured out upon it the best blood of the country;" and he could not be a mere partisan after that.

His work, in truth, was done. At the close of Johnson's administration he withdrew to private life, and gratified his love of roaming by a trip to Alaska, another to Mexico, and by a journey round the world. Everywhere he was received with the honor which was his due; and when his travels were over he returned to Auburn, and devoted himself to writing an account of his wanderings and the first chapters of his autobiography. In these employments a few months were passed, and then he died, quietly and peacefully, having just entered his seventy-second year.

Seward was a favorite of fortune. He was fortunate in his gifts, his surroundings, his successes, his career, his temperament, his friendships. He was peculiarly blessed in the last respect by having as a lifelong friend Thurlow Weed, one of the most astute and powerful politicians we have ever produced, who relieved Seward of many of the burdens of politics, and left him free to work out the principles they both had at heart. It was a rare chance which gave Seward such a friend, and he made the most of it, as he did of all his opportunities, after the fashion of successful people. Very few men have made themselves count for more than Seward, in proportion to their ability. This arose from his wonderful capacity for dealing with his fellow-men, from his robust common sense, and from his cautious firmness. The qualities, however, which made him great were his wisdom and his courage, and on these his place in history will rest. Apart from the military leaders, the great figure of the civil war is that of Abraham Lincoln. He will always stand preëminent, not only by his wisdom and his moral greatness, but by his hold upon the popular affection. He appealed to the hearts of the people both in his life and in his death. They loved him, because in him they saw a true and profoundly sympathetic representative of all that was best in themselves, and because he personified as no other man did the infinite pathos of the war. But among the statesmen who followed and sustained Lincoln Seward will occupy the foremost place. The memory of the adroit politician may perish, but that of the broad-minded statesman will endure. The subtleties of his arguments will fade, but his presentation of great principles will ever grow brighter. The champion of anti-masonry will be forgotten, but the man who first appealed to the " higher law " and who first described the " irrepressible conflict " will always be honored and remembered. We may read the epitaph which Seward chose for himself in the simple inscription on the tomb at Auburn, " He was faithful ; " and with this praise he was content. But history will also record and give high place to the calm wisdom, the loyal courage, and the undaunted spirit with which he defended the cause of freedom in a slave-holding Senate, and stood by the side of Lincoln through all the trials and perils of four years of civil war.

JAMES MADISON.

A DEBT of gratitude is due to Mr. Gay for his life of our fourth President.[1] He has opened the ponderous and marble jaws of the Rives biography, where Madison has been quietly inurned, and has thus permitted that distinguished statesman to revisit once more the glimpses of the moon. There is hardly a life in the series to which this volume belongs that so much needed to be written. Madison was one of the most conspicuous figures of his time. He held easily the second place in his party, and though he cannot be ranked with Washington, Hamilton, Jefferson, Adams, or Marshall, he was a statesman of a fine type, and followed close upon these great leaders. His services were important in themselves and lasting in their results. Yet with all this, and despite the many great offices which he held, Madison is neither familiar nor vivid to posterity. Hence the especial value of such an excellent biography as that by Mr. Gay.

That Madison, comparatively speaking, should be ill understood and imperfectly appreciated is not altogether due, by any means, to the fact that he fell into the hands of Mr. Rives, and thus be-

---

[1] *James Madison.* By Sydney Howard Gay. American Statesmen Series. Boston : Houghton, Mifflin & Co. 1884.

came the subject of one of the most solemn, learned, and highly respectable biographies ever penned by man. The real trouble is in Madison himself. He is an extremely difficult subject, historically speaking, as can be seen even in Mr. Gay's interesting volume. Mr. Gay writes with a skillful and practiced hand. There are very few better chapters in our history than those in which he has discussed the relations of parties and the French question during Washington's administration. But it is obvious that Mr. Gay has a keen sense of both the humorous and the picturesque; and, although it may be but fancy, one seems to detect a feeling of weariness in the author just because he possesses this gift. The narrative flows rapidly and closely, dealing more perhaps with public questions than with Madison, until the downfall of the Federalists. After that, although the merit of the work does not diminish in the least, the story goes forward with long strides, and five chapters suffice to cover the administrations of Jefferson and Madison and the twenty years of quiet which followed the latter's retirement from public life.

After all it is hardly matter for surprise that Mr. Gay should have become weary. It would have been strange indeed if he had not, for Madison, however highly we may rank his abilities and his services, is dry and serious to the last degree as a historical character. This arises chiefly from a defect which seems to have been common to the men of that day, but which reached its highest

development in Madison. Nothing is more striking in studying the period of the Revolution and of
the establishment of the government of the United
States than the absence of humor among the really
great men of that time. It is not that the mirth
of that age has lost its savor in ours. The humor
of Fielding and Smollett and the wit of Sheridan
appeal to us as keenly as to their contemporaries.
It is the same with our own great countryman,
Franklin, whose vein of strong, quiet humor has
delighted generations of readers. But among the
builders of the government of the United States
Gouverneur Morris appears to have been the solitary possessor of a genuine sense of humor, and his
speeches, as a natural consequence, seem to gleam
on the printed pages of constitutional debates in
singular contrast to the gray sobriety of his fel-
lows. Fisher Ames had humor, but it was of a
melancholy and sardonic sort, while the savage wit
of John Randolph and the effective sarcasms of
Quincy belong to a later period. John Adams
and in a less degree Jefferson are in very different
ways often unconsciously amusing, but here the
list must end. Although Hamilton had evidently
a hearty love of fun, no humor appears in his letters, yet he is vivid and picturesque by the force of
passion and the energy of a strong nature. This
is true, also, of such men as John Quincy Adams,
Timothy Pickering, and John Marshall.

Madison, however, had no such redeeming trait.
Mr. Rives cites as proof of Madison's humor a
letter written by Ellery and Madison jointly to

some fellow-members of Congress. **This** production is, at best, harmless fun, a species of labored
grinning through a horse-collar, and is, moreover,
obviously the work of Ellery from beginning to
end. There is no other testimony now in existence
on the strength of which Madison can be accused
of humor in any form. He was, in fact, utterly
destitute of that most valuable of human gifts, and
this lack was not at all supplied by high animal
spirits or by a strong and passionate temperament.
Madison, indeed, seems never to have had any
boyhood or youth. When he left college his health
was poor, he was very studious, very serious, and
very busy. He was only twenty-three when he
wrote to his friend Bradford, " Poetry, wit, criticism, plays, etc., captivated me much, but I began
to discover that they deserve but a small portion of
a mortal's time, and that something more substantial, more durable, and more profitable befits a
riper age." So this ripe young gentleman of
twenty-three freshened his mind by an extended
course of theological study, and then plunged into
that public career in which he was to play such a
useful and distinguished part. A man so constituted was, of course, cold and calm. Mr. Gay
says, in speaking of Madison's letter announcing
the victory of Yorktown: " Neither is there a
word of sympathetic warmth and patriotic fervor
which at that moment made the heart of a whole
people beat quicker at the news of a great victory." The disappointment he met with in his
first love affair tells the whole story. Madison

was then young, good - looking, a gentleman of
refined and cultivated manners, a scholar, and
already a highly distinguished man. He offered
everything that could tempt a woman's ambition or
gratify her pride. Yet Miss Floyd broke her en-
gagement with him to marry an obscure clergy-
man. Madison did not interest her, and posterity
has felt a good deal like Miss Floyd. Many years
later Madison married very happily, winning his
bride, as Mr. Rives tells us, by his "rare collo-
quial accomplishments," — a portentous sort of woo-
ing which explains perhaps Miss Floyd's feelings.

When, however, we pass from the qualities which
touch the heart or kindle the imagination Madison
appears very differently. He had some great and
many useful faculties. He was wonderfully indus-
trious and painstaking. He was not a versatile
man, and, except for an amateur fondness for natural history, he cared for nothing but politics and
the science of government, especially as applied to
the United States. With everything which could
by any possibility have the remotest bearing on
these topics he was thoroughly familiar, and his
familiarity was that of the scholar and not of the
man rapidly crammed for the occasion. The result was, that in his own field no one surpassed
him, and he still remains one of the best known
and most trusted expounders of our system of constitutional law.

As in constitutions and government, so in the
current political questions of his day, Madison
touched a good many without adorning them, but

never without manifesting a thorough knowledge and conveying much information to his hearers. He was eminently reasonable and practical, and although **not a** brilliant speaker, **he** was a convincing and effective leader in debate.   **The** chief causes of **his success, not only in** Congress **but elsewhere, were the general** soundness and **moderation of his views on all public questions.**   He rarely made **mistakes of judgment, except when from party** stress **he acted on the opinions of** other **people.** This wisdom, accompanied by a certain amount **of** shrewd foresight, was the source of the confidence that he enjoyed, and of all the popular strength he ever obtained.   But he had other and nobler qualities than these.   He was candid, conscientious, **just, and,** as **a rule,** high-minded.   Nothing **impresses one more in studying Madison's** correspondence **than the almost entire absence of personalities either hostile or** friendly.   He seems **never to have** undertaken to analyze character either **for his own** benefit or **for that of** his friends. He had **no** warm friendships **apparently, except** with Jefferson and Monroe, and he was equally **free** from bitter enmities.   If not a good lover, he was still less a good hater.   The strongest hostility he ever showed was toward Hamilton, whom he pursued **at one** period with **a** cold dislike of a rather **active and** ugly kind.   Yet in his later years his **inborn** sense **of justice** reasserted itself, and he **wrote of** Hamilton : **"That** he possessed intellectual powers of the first order and the moral qualifications of **integrity and honor in a captivating** degree have been decreed to him by a suffrage now universal. If his theory of government deviated from the republican standard, he had the candor to avow it, and the greater merit of co-operating faithfully in maturing and supporting a system which was not his choice."

The first public question that seems to have drawn Madison's attention was in regard to religious freedom. The petty persecutions of the Established Church in Virginia aroused his indignation, and he left his mark on the Virginian Bill of Rights in the clause which secured religious liberty. Toleration he resisted, as implying the right of the state to meddle with men's consciences, and he would accept nothing but absolute freedom. In this matter he not only won a victory in the Bill of Rights, but in later years he defeated finally various attempts to establish certain religious privileges in favor of the dominant church.

Madison entered public life at an early age, but it was a time when men developed rapidly, and he was always mature. He passed rapidly from the legislature to the council of Virginia, and thence to Congress at the close of the war. The soundness of his opinions and the ripeness of his wisdom in these first years of public life were most remarkable, and for all we can see now he was as skilled a statesman then as when he laid down the Presidency after forty years of public life. Not only on the matter of religious freedom, but on other public questions in regard to which popular opinion fluctuated constantly, he was ever just,

steady, and true. In the councils of his own State
he fought against the curse of paper money, re-
vised and condensed the laws, strove to have the
treaty kept in regard to British debts, and labored
zealously for intelligent commercial legislation and
for all other useful reforms. In Congress he
worked day and night to overcome the hopeless
difficulties of the confederation. He grappled with
the debt and with the revenue, and sought to give
strength to the imbecile central government of
which he was a part. In regard to the Missis-
sippi he held right opinions and took enlarged
views at a time when there was a strong pressure
to sacrifice our interests in the great river for the
sake of peace with Spain. In that matter Madison showed plenty of courage, as he usually did
when he felt sure he was right. This was conspicu-
ously the case also in regard to slavery. In 1785
he wrote: " Another of my wishes is to depend as
little as possible on the labor of slaves." The system of human bondage was indeed odious to his
gentle and liberal nature, and he was courageous
in his treatment of it. He would have liked to
abolish the " peculiar institution," but there he
shrank back, probably because he saw that it was
a task beyond any man's strength. Still his influence was always against it, and when the abolition petitions appeared in the first Congress he
wished to have those petitions respectfully referred
and then rejected after a simple presentation of
the constitutional objections. This was advanced
ground to take at that day, and if the South had

followed Madison's advice they would have fared
much better than by trying to strangle the right
of petition and thus arousing a spirit which never
slumbered nor slept until the whole infamous system went down in utter ruin.

Madison's chief title to fame and gratitude
comes, however, from his share in forming the
Constitution of the United States. No one did
more in this momentous work, and only two others
as much as he. From the time when they first
came together in Congress Hamilton and Madison labored with equal zeal for the establishment
of a better government. They saw the fatal defects in the fading system of the confederation.
They were imbued with the same ideas as to the
proper remedies. One at the North, the other at
the South, they reached out their hands to each
other, and backed by the quiet but masterful influence of Washington they finally succeeded, and
carried through one of the greatest triumphs of
modern statesmanship. To Madison in Virginia,
alert and attentive, came the first opportunity.
With great adroitness he seized the slender chance
held out by the conferences of Virginia and Maryland, and obtained the call for the Annapolis convention. Hamilton responded in an instant. The
convention met. It was an unpromising beginning, but it gave Hamilton and Madison the point
for the lever by which they could move their world.
They pried with all their might to raise the inert
mass of the States, and the result was the convention at Philadelphia. Side by side they fought for

the adoption of a strong and energetic government, and when the Constitution was completed they together wrote " The Federalist," and in their respective States fought two of the decisive and most desperate battles of the whole struggle in behalf of union and national existence.

The new government was established, the machinery began to move, and then Madison and Hamilton separated, never to meet again except as foes. This was the turning point of Madison's life, and Mr. Gay has analyzed the question which it raises with both skill and justice. In his old age Madison was much nettled by charges of inconsistency, and passed a good deal of time in showing that he was always perfectly consistent. Why he should have been so sensitive on this point it is not easy to see. He had never " ratted," nor had he ever sold himself or betrayed his party from mean motives. But his change of front was certainly marked, and the inconsistency between his natural opinions and his public actions from 1790 to 1800 is strikingly obvious. Madison was by nature and instinct a " Federalist." Indeed, it was he who established, if he did not coin, the word itself. He was a cautious man, with no popular gifts or attractions, a lover of a strong, well-ordered government, not given to experiments or to new ideas, the very reverse of sentimental, and not at all imbued with the notions about humanity then swarming out of France. Thus formed by nature, he acted all his life as one of the leaders of the Democratic party, became its second choice for the Presidency and a recognized exponent of the Jeffersonian theories, which then constituted Democracy in the party sense. A very brief comparison of Madison's opinions before 1789 with those which he advocated afterwards shows the extent of the change which he made in his course as a public man.

Madison believed in the first place that property should be represented, and that manhood suffrage ought to control one branch of the legislature and property suffrage the other. This theory he advocated both in youth and old age, and apparently never changed his mind about it. All that can be said on this point is that Madison's view was certainly not democratic. He believed in a strong central government, and wrote and said over and over again that he considered an absolute negative on all State laws whatsoever essential to any effective system. He proposed to give this vast power either to Congress, the President, or the national judiciary. Hamilton has been criticised always for his proposition to give the appointments of governors of States to the President, but this was merely reaching the veto power in another way. In details they differed, but Madison and Hamilton agreed in the fundamental point, that the central government must control absolutely the legislation of the States. If a more centralizing theory than this of Madison's existed it was not put forward, and it reads oddly enough when placed side by side with the Virginia resolutions of '98. In regard to finance, the point on which everything then hinged, Madison believed in the fullest

provision for the debt; he was one of the earliest
supporters of a permanent revenue; he favored
funding; he opposed discrimination among holders
of the domestic debt, and in 1783 and 1785 he
argued strongly in favor of the principle of assumption of the State debts. In 1787, when the
work of forming the Constitution fairly began, we
are able to trace his opinions very clearly. He
wrote to Randolph that the individual independence of the States was incompatible with the idea
of an aggregate sovereignty; he defended the negative on the States, and wished to extend national
supremacy to the courts. In another letter he described the party adverse to the Constitution as
bent on the dissolution of the Union. A little
later he wrote that equality of votes among the
States must cease in order to secure a *national*
instead of a *federal* government, and he also declared against the ratification of the new system by
the States, and wished to have it referred directly
to the people.

In the debates of the convention Madison's
national and centralizing principles come out even
more strongly and plainly. He urged three years
as the proper term for members of Congress, dwelt
on the instability of republics and the danger that
the House would overwhelm the Senate, and opposed the proposition to restrict the right of origi-
nating money bills to the popular branch. After
the introduction of the so-called New Jersey plan
Hamilton made his great speech of June 18, one
principal object being to counteract the weakening

effect of the system outlined by Mr. Patterson.
The next day Madison followed Hamilton with a
strong speech in the same direction. A little later
he declared that there was no objection in principle to one great republic, but merely considerations of inconvenience and impracticability. He
was not in favor of forbidding members of Congress to hold other offices, and he advocated a
property qualification for electors of the Senators,
for whom he thought a term of nine years none too
long. In another speech he urged that the true
policy for the small States was in a system which
would reduce the States to the level of counties.
He believed in a strong executive, opposed zealously the equality of votes in the Senate, and on
the question of representation employed the language of Hamilton in regard to large and small
States. Indeed, at a later day he went further
than Hamilton, arguing boldly that the freeholders
would be the safest depositaries of republican
liberty. He was also against giving the States any
power to control the election of congressmen; he
favored placing the State militia in the power of
the general government; and he believed in taxing
exports.

On these principles he continued to act after the
adjournment of the convention. He contributed
to " The Federalist," referring constantly to the
British Constitution as a standard, and then returned to Virginia to lead the fight for the new
system. Defeated for the Senate through Henry's
exertions, he succeeded after a sharp contest with

Monroe in securing an election to the lower House. In the new Congress he easily took the lead, and there is no change apparent in his attitude throughout the first session. Indeed, he continued to write to Jefferson and his other friends that the danger still to be apprehended was from the strength of the States and the feebleness of the general government.

Madison's change dates from the beginning of the second session of the first Congress; in other words, from the appearance of the report on the Public Credit. The turning about was complete and decided. Madison did not go gradually into opposition because he did not fancy the scheme of policy developed by Hamilton. In his later years he was fond of thinking that this was the case; but in reality he opposed it step by step, and from the very outset. If it had devolved on Madison to mark out a policy for the administration, there is no reason to suppose that it would have differed in principle from the one actually undertaken. Yet the very instant Hamilton began to strike out the bold and masterly policy which was to convert the dry clauses of the Constitution into a strong and living organism Madison began to resist. There was no difference of opinion as to the foreign debt, but on the domestic debt Madison took a position in favor of discrimination, and produced a scheme as impracticable as could well be conceived. The sharpness of the change is best shown by the fact that Hamilton in arguing against discrimination in his report found his best support in quoting Madison's own words on that subject sent forth to the country some years before in the address to the States.

It is easy to show the sudden and complete change made by Madison. It is much more difficult to account for it. His action, as is usually the case, was probably due to a variety of motives. In the first place, there were two points on which he was consistent throughout his life. Despite his national views and his labors for the Constitution he was always in the last resort a Virginian first, a Southerner next, and an American last. In that day and generation there was nothing either peculiar or discreditable about this. With the exception of Washington, who by largeness of mind rose above all local prejudices, and of Hamilton, who was born without them and was too broad to acquire them, all the men of that day were in a greater or less degree sectional. It was human nature, that was all. They loved their States, which had always existed for them, and they had only a theoretic and reasoned devotion to the Union, which was a thing of yesterday. When their party or their section was in power they were strongly national; when they were in the minority the reverse was the case. Madison was as fervent in his state feeling as it was possible for him to be in anything. With his calm sense he saw clearly, as few others did, that the real contest in the convention was not between large and small States, but between the North and South, between freedom and slavery. When the new government began to move he saw the financial **policy** enriching **the North**, and not the South ; and he saw, too, the **rise** of the North to political power under Washington. Here was one powerful reason for opposition.

The other point on which Madison **never** swerved **was in regard to** France.   **He belonged to the school which had a deep** sentimental **prejudice in favor of that country.   He showed this feeling** strongly **in the debates of 1782–83, and he never** could get rid **either of his prejudice or of the old** colonial habit of clinging to foreign politics **for** guidance and inspiration.   This was also the view of Jefferson, and speedily became that of the party which he and Madison formed and led.

On the other hand the Federalists, **as Mr. Gay points out, were the** first American **party.**   Their **policy was to avoid any connection with any power across the water, and to treat all alike,** allowing the **dead past to bury its dead.   Such an** attitude was **odious to Madison.   He and all the rest of his** friends undertook **to say that they resisted the** Federalists because the Federalists **wished** to **favor** England.   **In reality they resisted them** because the Federalists were not willing to enter into **close** connection with France.   In course of time, under **the** stress **of** party warfare and with minds distorted **by** hatred of the French Revolution, the **Federalists became as colonial in** politics as their opponents, **and** talked about England as Jefferson used to talk about **France.   But this was in** their **last and worst days, and while the** Federalists **were** led **by Washington, Hamilton, and Adams**

they were a purely national and American party.
His French prejudices before many years elapsed
drove Madison into the most eager partisanship of
which he was capable, but when he first changed
they did not, of course, play a very strong part.

Other influences, however, were at work in 1790.
Virginia, as Madison had reason to know, was, in
the main, anti-Federalist. Henry had defeated
him for the Senate, and then nearly snuffed out
his political light by making a district which would
not send him to Congress, thus anticipating by
twenty years the ingenious scheme which bears the
name of Elbridge Gerry. Madison loved public
life. He cared, indeed, for nothing else. He pre-
ferred, other things being equal, to be in sympathy
with his State, and that preference was sharpened
when lack of sympathy portended a serious check.
It was a case where sentiment fortified by interest
clashed with well-reasoned opinions, and the former
prevailed.

The final impulse which spurred Madison to
turn sharply a corner which he was surely and
steadily approaching was of a more personal kind.
He and Hamilton had fought the battle of the
Constitution side by side. Then the latter came
into power, and with bold and resolute hand drove
along a vigorous and far-reaching policy. Madison was deeply ambitious in his calm, reticent way.
He had done more than any one except Washington and Hamilton to build up the Constitution.
That done he went to Congress because he felt
that there better than anywhere else he could make

the experiment a success. To his great surprise,
he found the task taken from his hands. The
guiding force of the new government came from
the administration, not from Congress. That he
should feel disappointed and nettled was natural
enough, and his irritation turned against the man
who seemed to be doing the work and reaping the
harvest of glory which belonged to himself. To
say that it was merely personal envy of another's
success which led Madison into opposition would
be unjust. Yet it is at least certain that from the
moment of the appearance of the first report on
the Public Credit Madison began to be hostile to
its author. His feelings strengthened fast, and he
soon showed toward Hamilton a cold jealousy and
a frigid but active hatred which led him into a
course of action foreign to his real nature and unworthy of his pure character and well-balanced
mind. Personal hostility urged him on, and his
admiration for Jefferson, the one strong friendship
of his life, impelled him in the same direction.

Thus, from a mixture of motives, Madison ar-
rayed himself in opposition to the men, the party,
and the measures with which he naturally sympathized. Local associations, State pride, sectional
feeling, sentiment, interest, personal friendship,
and personal hostility all combined to the same
end. Once started he moved quickly enough.
Support of discrimination in the domestic debt
was followed by resistance to assumption. Not
long before, he had advanced and defended the
principle of assumption, and the motives at work

within him come out curiously in his new attitude on this important question. In 1790 he writes that he is not opposed to the principle of assumption, but that it bears hard on Virginia. In all his fierce resistance to this measure the fact that it did not profit Virginia was the controlling influence. So in regard to the site of the Federal city, in which he took an intense interest. He discussed the situation of the capital as if the fate of the nation hung upon it, and dilated continually upon the infamous combinations of the Eastern and Middle States to deprive the South of this advantage and honor. He had a keen dislike of New England, and this feeling was concentrated in a curious way upon John Adams, of whom he always spoke in a bitter and contemptuous way for which it is difficult to find adequate cause, except that he regarded that sturdy fighter as peculiarly representative of the North and East.

Madison was not fitted by nature for a partisan, but unsuccessful opposition made him one, and for years he opposed, without distinction, everything emanating from the administration or its friends, a course in which he was much aided by his devotion to France, whose affairs soon came to play a leading part in our politics. He easily adopted all Jefferson's jargon about " Anglicans, monarchists, and a corrupt squadron." He opposed the National Bank as unconstitutional, and assailed Hamilton's report on Manufactures as in every way wrong. When Genet arrived he was at first delighted by his pranks, and then he mourned over that gentle-

man's follies as serious **misfortunes**. He was opposed to the neutrality policy, and when Hamilton
defended **it as** " Pacificus " he replied as " Helvi-
dius " **to those** " who hate our Republican govern-
ment and **the** French Revolution." It is pleasant
to think how impossible it **now** would be to couple
**the United States in that way with any foreign na-
tion.** Yet **Madison found no difficulty in doing it,**
and **Mr. Rives declares that these essays of** " Hel-
vidius " **crushed Hamilton.** In view of this fact it
is not a little curious **to note** that when **Hamilton**
wrote " Camillus " and Jefferson invited Madison
to again enter the lists that victorious gentleman
prudently declined.

The nature of the opposition to which **Madison
committed himself** comes out most strongly in certain **personal matters.** Jefferson **has** repelled with
indignation the idea that **there was** anything political in Freneau's case. **Madison is** much franker.
He wanted an opposition newspaper, and **while** he
helped **to get** subscriptions he wished **also** to encourage **the** editor **with a government office.** For
this reason he was instrumental **in** bringing **Fre-**
neau to Philadelphia and **to the State** Department.
Mr. Rives, with Virginian grandiloquence, calls
Freneau a " rare genius," **but Madison,** one may
venture to think, considered him simply a useful
and clever journalist, and as such employed **him.**

Setting up **an** opposition newspaper was **harm-**
less enough, but **the attempt** to ruin Hamilton was
a contemptible business, which was well punished
by **the** ridiculous **way** in **which it broke down.**

Madison in fact never appeared to less advantage than when drawing hostile resolutions and putting forward a tool like Giles to make an ugly and ruinous attack upon a man whom he acknowledged in his old age to be of captivating integrity. All that can be said for him on this point is that Jefferson, and not he, was the real originator of the precious scheme. In the same vein, however, he wrote of Hamilton, in 1795: "It is pompously announced in the newspapers that poverty drives him back to the Bar for a livelihood." Whether pompously announced or not, it was the truth, and the sneer came with poor grace from a man who could retire to a plantation and be supported by the labor of a drove of slaves. The hatred of opposition, however, reached a higher point even than this, for in 1796 Madison rejoiced that the House refused to adjourn for half an hour on February 22d in order to pay their respects to Washington. At this same period, too, he adopted his party's trick of sorrowing over Washington's weakness and the manner in which that great man fell a prey to designing persons, which was a kind of contemptuous pity a thousand times more offensive than any direct attack.

Thus it was that Madison, gentle and just by nature, was carried on from point to point, and was involved in deeper and deeper inconsistencies. He assailed Hamilton's debt, but resisted all plans to reduce it, especially when the taxes proposed seemed likely to reach Virginia. He hated England and wished to attack her; but when Sedg-

wick, leading the Federalists, proposed to arm he
resisted their measures and impugned their motives. He wanted a navy, but was opposed to
beginning to build one, and thought it best to buy
peace from the pirates of Algiers. He sneered at
the whiskey rebellion, and sought excuses for the
French in the disgraceful X. Y. Z. affair. It may
be said that all this was simply ordinary political
opposition, which is true enough. The trouble is
that it was not work for which Madison was fitted,
and that he did not rest here, but allowed his
opposition to culminate at last in an act which sat
heavy on his soul down to the day of his death.
In 1798 he wrote the famous Virginia resolutions,
and the next year reaffirmed their doctrine, in his
report on the replies from the other States. It
boots not to inquire whether Jefferson consulted
him as to the Kentucky resolutions. Madison
strenuously denied that the god of his political
idolatry had used the fatal words "nullify or nullification," but the tell-tale manuscript showed that
he was mistaken, and that Jefferson had the honor
of first using that famous expression. The word
was really of little consequence, although Madison
rested his own defense on the fact that he did not
employ it. His word was "interpose," and he saw
so vast a difference, so great a gulf fixed between
that and "nullification," that he fought upon this
theme against his South Carolina imitators of 1830
with all the vigor of his early days. It was vain
quibbling. The Hartford convention only wished
to "interpose," but Madison had no question as to

what the Hartford convention intended. Their
"interposition" meant to him nullification and im-
pending secession. His own resolution meant the
same thing, and with all his subtlety of distinction
he could not change the meaning. He urged "in-
terposing" the power and rights of the States to
check the general government, and, by whatever
fine name it might be called, the road he pointed
out was the highway of separatism and led straight
to secession. There was no distinction in principle between the Virginia resolutions and the South
Carolina movement as Madison contended, but
there was a wide difference between the Madison
of 1798 expounding other men's separatist views,
and the Madison of 1830 explaining his own national principles. Had he really believed in the
doctrines of '98 he never would have tried to excuse and explain them away.

These resolutions marked high water in the
change which began for Madison in 1790. With
the new century his party came into power. From
that time a contrary movement set in and Madison
moved back steadily to his former ground, until
in his old age he was again the statesman of the
constitutional convention. It is curious to mark
this reverse process. Madison never needed the
sobering influence which great responsibility brings
to all men, but power killed the party spirit which
with him was at best but a carefully cultivated
exotic. During Jefferson's two terms Madison,
trusted and beloved as he was by his chief, played
a purely subordinate part. Jefferson was a polit-

ical autocrat, and his administration was wholly
his own. Madison did the work of his department as he did all work, faithfully, conscientiously,
and well. His state papers are dignified and able,
and so is his elaborate pamphlet on the British
doctrine in regard to neutrals. But his letters are
colorless during this time, and the foreign policy
was that of Jefferson.

Madison, however, waited patiently to some
purpose. When Jefferson was ready to retire he
named as his successor his faithful friend and Secretary of State, and the well-drilled party accepted
the edict without a murmur. It was the goal of
Madison's ambition, but even when he grasped the
glittering prize of the Presidency he must have
felt that it had its drawbacks. There was a
strange irony in fate's thrusting Madison into command when the ship of state was tossing on the
stormiest seas she has ever faced except in 1861.
Madison was preëminently a man of peace, and
here he was on the verge of war, England and
France snarling at him on one side, and a hot-
headed war party goading him on the other. He
kept on clutching at peace with desperate hands,
but all in vain. It would be useless and indeed
impossible to follow here the tedious twistings of
our foreign relations during Madison's first term.
All that concerns us is to note the way in which
he plunged on from one Federalist measure to another, embracing once more the principles which
were really congenial to him, and which he had
passed ten years of his life in reviling. By 1811

he was ready to accept the hated bank, and a few years later he signed the bill establishing a new one, and wrote that the State banks ought to unite with the National Bank in restoring health to the currency. Obviously Hamilton had some method in his madness on that point at least.

Then dangers of foreign hostilities began to draw nearer, and the clamors of the war party grew ever louder. Yet in the spring of 1812 we find Madison sneering at Congress because they talked of war and at the same time would neither raise a sufficient army, nor build a navy, nor strengthen the executive. This too smacked sadly of Federalism. Madison, of course, wished and hoped to avoid war, but he was compelled to choose between that and political ruin. Whether Clay and others went to him and threatened to deprive him of the nomination or not is of no great consequence. Madison did not need to be told that if he could not lead the war party some one else would. He fell in with the dominant element of his party and went to war. He liked it about as well as Bob Acres liked dueling, and once in he worked night and day to get out. The Federalists used to call it "Madison's war," and a grimmer satire was never uttered. There was not a Federalist to be found who hated the war half as much as the unfortunate gentleman whose name it bore.

As might have been expected, Madison made a very poor war President. His heart was not in the thing in the first place, and, moreover, with all his great abilities and fine qualities he was not a fighting man. Still, he struggled along as best he could, and finally made peace, a wise peace no doubt, but concluded on terms which made the Jay treaty and still more the Monroe treaty, so cavalierly rejected by Jefferson, seem the highest triumphs of vigorous diplomacy. It is just possible that there may have been moments when Madison thought that after all Washington and Hamilton were not so wholly weak and foolish as he had declared them to be when they accepted the Jay treaty and persuaded the country to do the same.

So the war closed, greatly to the relief of Madison, who then proceeded to sign the Bank Bill, and also the first avowedly protective tariff. One cannot help wondering if he remembered, in performing the latter act, his observations upon a certain report on Manufactures. Probably he did not, for he was now acting in consonance with that national policy which was natural to him. The Jeffersonian theory of a simple government, without armies or navies, or loans, or anything else in particular, had broken down under the stress of circumstances. Madison, relieved from this theory, was now able to proceed as he liked, and his administration, after the Treaty of Ghent, was wise, moderate, and successful. He had managed to get rid of a number of annoying persons who had been bequeathed to him by Jefferson, and his last years of office were a time of well-earned peace.

When his second term ended he sought a dignified retirement on his estate, and there, among his friends and his books, he passed a happy, useful, and honored old age. His keen love of political and constitutional questions could only die with him, and, in a quiet way, by means of letters, he continued to take an important part in public affairs. He threw the great weight of his name, and all the force of his influence, in favor of the protective policy. Abstractly, he may have thought that free trade was best. Practically, he believed that protection was essential to the United States. In a word, he did not differ in practice from Hamilton on this great question, and if he could have then renewed his youth he would have been a stanch Whig. When the nullification of South Carolina shook the country he came forward nobly and strongly for the Union, and did all in his power to undo the teachings of the Virginia and Kentucky resolutions. In the soft, clear sunset of his life his sectional prejudices dropped away, and he fixed his hopes and his affections upon the Union. To love the Union was, indeed, his last message to his countrymen.

Madison's political career is, in some ways, a very curious one, but it can be summed up in few words. By nature and reason he was a Federalist and a nationalist. By circumstances he became a Democrat, and at one time a separatist. He was entirely faithful to the party which he espoused, but he was not in full and entire sympathy with it. The result was, that he founded no school and had no personal following. The party which he led honored and trusted him, and it is to their honor and credit that they did so. But they neither loved him nor sympathized with him. The party with which he really sympathized opposed him throughout his life. Politically speaking, he was a lonely man, and that loneliness has continued until to-day. No party has placed him among its heroes for stated or occasional worship. He seems to stand aloof in history as he did in life, respected and honored by all, loved and followed by none. With such a nature as Madison's it could not well be otherwise, and his career was possible only to a man as cold, as conscientious, and as liberal as he was. He was a poor partisan, but a great and useful statesman. He did some unworthy things, he made mistakes, like the rest of humanity, but his abilities and his character are an honor to his country and to his State. Statues may not rise to him in the market-place, political parties may not enshrine him as a patron saint, but by his labors in the establishment of the government and the Constitution of the United States, and by a pure and dignified character and career, he has built himself a monument more enduring than any of brass or marble.

GOUVERNEUR MORRIS.

GOUVERNEUR MORRIS is by no means so well known to the present generation as he ought to be.[1] Perhaps it would be more accurate to say that he has not been and is not justly appreciated. If, however, we turn to M. Taine's great work on the French Revolution, we find that he relies on Morris as one of the best and most penetrating observers of that terrible convulsion, and places him at the head of a small group of men like Arthur Young, Malouet, and Mallet du Pan, who alone were able to record clear and dispassionate judgments in that

[1] This article first appeared in *The Atlantic Monthly* for April, 1886. At that time Mr. Sparks's three volumes of memoirs, letters, and fragments of the diary were all that we had to tell us about Gouverneur Morris. Since then Miss Morris has published a new edition of her grandfather's diary. Much more attractive in form than the Sparks edition and somewhat fuller, the diary in its last form is still incomplete, and adds but little to our knowledge of the writer. Since 1886 also Mr. Roosevelt's admirable biography of Morris has appeared, and given for the first time an adequate picture of the man and his services. In the presence of these publications the first sentence of this sketch becomes very inexact. It was quite true, however, when it was written, and so I let it stand. I reprint the essay itself, because Gouverneur Morris, both as statesman and man, has not thus far at least been written about or discussed beyond his deserts, and even this imperfect sketch may help toward a juster estimate of an important and picturesque figure in the history of the United States.

dizzy time, for the benefit of posterity. The comments of Mr. Morris, thus rescued from his biography and brought before a wide public by M. Taine, already have attracted attention elsewhere, and a recent article in " Macmillan's **Magazine** " show how striking his criticisms and narratives really are. Such a prophet should never be without honor in his own country, and now that he is winning admiration in England and France, perhaps it would not be amiss to refresh our own memories in regard to him.

It is not to be wondered at that M. **Taine** and others find so much that is admirable in Gouverneur Morris, for in him many high qualities met in a rare combination. **A man of the world and of society, a wit,** philosopher, and **fine** gentleman, he was also a bold **and ardent patriot, an able** and most **practical statesman, a** distinguished lawyer, and a **successful** manager of large **business** affairs. He played a conspicuous **part among the many** eminent **men of his day and country, but in one** respect he differs from them **all.** He had a **sharp** wit, a strong sense **of** humor, **and a capacity for** amusing **satire** which **are to be found** in all **his** writings. **If we except Franklin, who** was of an **earlier** generation, Gouverneur **Morris** holds **in this** respect a lonely preëminence among **his** friends and **contemporaries.** The leaders of **our** revolutionary **and** constitutional **period** were, **it must be con**fessed, judging **from** their letters and journals, somewhat ponderous. **Now** and then **we** find **a** moment **when we can** laugh at them, **but Morris is** almost the **only one with whom we laugh or smile**

in sympathy. This is enough of itself to make us
hold him in remembrance, but at the same time he
was far more than merely an amusing companion
or a writer of clever letters.

He was born in 1752, a cadet in a family which
had been distinguished for two or three generations
in the colonies, not only for public service and high
office, but for certain quaint eccentricities and for
unusual acuteness in discussion and power in argument. A bright boy at college, fond of Shake-
speare, and a maker of rhymes and verses, he grad-
uated with honor, and delivered a Commencement
oration on Wit and Beauty. A little later, on taking his degree of A. M., he pronounced a discourse
on Love, and both these boyish productions displayed, despite their florid style, a command of
language and a vigorous imagination which were
destined to stand their author in good stead in the
years to come. His patrimony was small, only
some £2,000, and he had his way to make in the
world; but his was not a nature to be discouraged,
and he faced the future cheerfully and boldly. He
often said in after life that in his intercourse with
other men he had never experienced the sensation
of fear, inferiority, or awkwardness. Armed with
this easy self-confidence, he applied himself fear-
lessly to the task of winning success. He studied
law, wrote at the age of eighteen against the popular plan of issuing bills of credit (an early evidence
of his financial talents) and in 1771 was duly admitted to the bar. He was soon in active practice,
and as the times grew more stirring solemnly de-

clared that he disliked politics. His natural humor
made him laugh at both parties, and his Tory con-
nections, soon to become a thorn in his side, led
him to favor a union with England and the concession to Parliament of the right to regulate trade.

But with all his sense of the ridiculous and his
tendency to find food for satire in his fellow-men,
Morris was no Gallio. The ministerial side was
impossible to a young, generous, ardent spirit, and
in 1775 he was a member of the Provincial Congress of New York, where he at once took a leading part in organizing resistance and preparing for
war. He advocated a continental currency, and
his report on that subject was sent to Congress.
He served on all the leading committees, and in
1776 made a speech for independent government
which was replete with sarcasm and full of ability.
From a letter of that time we learn how strongly
he felt then, and how completely the early careless-
ness and merriment had vanished in the face of
stern events. He wrote to his mother : —

" What may be the event of the present war it is
not in man to determine. Great revolutions of empire are seldom achieved without much human ca-
lamity ; but the worst which can happen is to fall
on the last bleak mountain of America, and he who
dies there, in defense of the injured rights of mankind, is happier than his conqueror, more beloved
by mankind, more applauded by his own heart."

The spirit of the man was equal to his words.
He took a leading part in framing the constitution
of New York, and even then, in the din of war,

strove to insert a clause abolishing slavery. He served on the Council of Safety, which held control until the new government was set in motion, and his energy, zeal, and organizing power were felt in all directions. No one was more active than he in sustaining the army and doing all in his power to assist our generals, especially Schuyler, who seemed to Morris, as to many others, both then and since, to be the victim of injustice. He strongly believed, in fact, that a campaign of obstruction was best for us, and he felt from the outset that in this way the English expedition from Canada could be most surely ruined. Even on so grave a subject, however, his humor crops out, and while he is solemnly arguing as to the campaign against Burgoyne he wrote : —

" I am also told that the Indians are determined to take up the hatchet for us. If this be true, it would be infinitely better to wear away the enemy's army by a scrupulous and polite attention, than to violate the rules of decorum and the laws of hospitality by making an attack upon strangers in our own country."

In 1778 he was promoted to a seat in the Continental Congress, and although only twenty-six years old he came forward there with the same ease as on the smaller stage of New York. This was chiefly due, of course, to his ability, but also in part to his really remarkable capacity for rapid and effective work. He was on the committee to visit Washington at Valley Forge ; he urged the plan of provision for the officers of the army ; he drew reports on the condition of the Union, on a plan for a treasury board and for a medical department. In the course of this work he became intimate with Greene, and formed a warm friendship with Washington, which continued unabated through life. In the miserable cabals against the general, Morris made determined war upon the schemers, and his indignation breaks out sharply in a letter to Washington: —

"You have enemies. It is happy for you that you have. A man of sentiment has not so much honor, as the vulgar suppose, in resigning life and fortune for the service of his country. He does not value them as highly as the vulgar do. Would he give the highest evidence, let him sacrifice his feelings. In the history of last winter, posterity will do you justice."

Political and personal conflicts, however, did not turn him from his labors. From his busy pen came the report on Lord North's conciliatory bills, an address on the treaties with France, a sketch of the negotiations with the commissioners, a draft of instructions for Franklin, a pamphlet on our finances to be presented to the French court, and finally, in 1779, a draft of instructions as to making peace. These manifold and eminent services did not, apparently, satisfy his constituents. Unjust prejudices and suspicions on account of his Tory relatives, so strong that he did not dare even to visit his mother when she was critically ill, together with charges that he neglected the local interests of New York, especially in regard to Vermont, prevailed against him, and he was not reëlected when his term expired.

He thereupon moved to Philadelphia, to practice
his profession, write upon finance, and attack the
dangerous and futile legal-tender and maximum
laws. Just after his retirement from Congress,
he was thrown from his phaeton and severely injured. By the rash advice of his surgeon his leg
was amputated, a severe trial to an active, energetic
man; but he bore his misfortune with the cheerful philosophy which was always his most marked
characteristic, and jested about it even in the
midst of his suffering. He was visited by one of
those consoling friends of the kind familiar to
every one, who held forth about the good effects of
such a dispensation, and the check which it would
be to dangerous pleasures and dissipations. When
he had concluded Mr. Morris said, " My good sir,
you argue the matter so handsomely, and point out
so clearly the advantages of being without legs,
that I am almost tempted to part with another."
To another sympathizer he said, " Oh, sir, the loss
is much less than you imagine; I shall doubtless be
a steadier man with one leg than with two." The
plain wooden leg with which he supplied his griev-
ous and painful loss, if tradition may be believed,
was once used to good purpose by his ready wit.
In the stormy time in Paris, when Terror ruled,
and not even a foreign minister was safe, Morris's
chariot was one day stopped by an angry mob, and
immediate violence was threatened. Morris thrust
out his wooden leg, and cried, " I am an American! See what I suffered in the war for liberty
and independence ! " The mob was converted by

such ocular demonstration of patriotic suffering, and drew their intended victim home in triumph instead of hanging him to a lamp-post.

Great as the misfortune was, however, it did not even at the moment diminish Morris's energy or depress his spirits. When his friend Robert Morris was appointed to the charge of our disordered finances, he took the position of assistant secretary, and contributed largely to the work which did so much to save the American cause. He also, in addition to his heavy public duties, carried on a large law practice, both in the courts and before the legislature, where he made one of his most brilliant and in its day famous speeches, concluding with an apostrophe to William Penn, which moved his hearers to tears, — a feat that seems hardly compatible with the theme. During all this period, too, he wrote much for the press, and took an active part in politics. He drew a report on coinage, and published a pamphlet on our trade with the French West Indies. He urged an opposition to the congressional instructions to follow blindly the wishes of France, and in season and out of season advocated the claims of the army. Like all friends of the soldiers at that time, he was accused of being a monarchist, — a singularly unjust charge against a man whose first maxim was that government must conform to the habits and character of the people, and who greatly feared an attempt to introduce monarchy, "because it did not consist with our taste and temper." At the same time, like all the ablest and strongest

men in that period of feebleness and solution, he
worked ardently for a better and stronger union.
In 1784 he wrote to Jay : —

"A national spirit is the natural result of national existence ; and although some of the present
generation may feel colonial opposition of opinion, yet this generation will die away and give
place to a race of Americans."

In the same spirit, and in almost his first speech
in the constitutional convention to which he was
chosen as a delegate from Pennsylvania, and in
which be played a most conspicuous part, he declared : —

"I come here as a representative of America.
I flatter myself that I come here in some degree as
a representative of the whole human race ; for the
whole human race will be affected by the proceed-
ings of this convention. I wish gentlemen to extend
their views beyond the present moment of time, —
beyond the narrow limits of place from which they
derive their political origin." Again he said, with
"something like prophetic strain," "This country
must be united. If persuasion does not unite it,
the sword will."

No man did better work in the great task of
forming the Constitution than Morris, and from
his hand came the final draft, rounded and polished,
which embodied the principles forged slowly in
weeks of debate. He of course belonged to the
party which favored a vigorous central government.
He opposed bitterly equality of votes in the Senate, and sought to weaken the rights of the States.

He wished a President for life, elected by the people, and also a Senate with a life tenure. Property, he believed, should be represented, and the suffrage conferred only on freeholders; maintaining, also, that persons of foreign birth should be ineligible to office. What few others then perceived his keen mind detected, that the South was determined to secure a majority and rule at all hazards, and he fought fiercely against slave representation. Slavery, however, aroused his enmity on much broader grounds than those of political power. He had already striven for abolition in the New York convention, and he renewed the struggle on the national field. On moving to insert the word "free" before "inhabitants" he made a speech of great force and eloquence, beginning : —

"Much will depend on this point. I will never concur in upholding domestic slavery. It is a nefarious institution. It is the curse of heaven on the States where it prevails." Nothing shows the breadth of view, the far-reaching vision, and the generous spirit of the man better than his relentless and outspoken resistance to the malignant system which was destined to bring the country so near to utter ruin and dissolution.

After all was over he expressed in a letter to a friend in France his opinion of the great work on which he had been engaged, and it would be difficult to find a juster estimate in the year 1788 of the Constitution, then struggling for an opportunity to live, than this of Morris, with its characteristic touch of satire. He wrote : —

" You will long ere this have seen the Constitution proposed for the United States. This paper
has been the subject of infinite investigation, dis-
putation, and declamation. While some have
boasted it as a work from Heaven, others have
given it a less righteous origin. I have many reasons to believe that it was the work of plain, honest men, and such I think it will appear. Faulty
it must be, for what is perfect? But if adopted,
experience will, I believe, show that its faults are
just the reverse of what they are supposed to be."

Soon after these lines were written he sailed for
Europe to attend to certain business interests, little
dreaming of the long absence from home that was
before him, or of the great events in which he was
to be an actor and which he was to describe so
vividly in the diary then begun.

He arrived in Paris on the 3d of February, 1789,
and the first two persons he visited were Jefferson
and Lafayette. Of the latter, of whom he was very
fond, he curtly says, " Lafayette is full of politics;
he appears to be too republican for the genius of
his country." At the very outset he had doubts
and suspicions as to the soundness and wisdom of
the revolutionary party, and these feelings and
opinions strengthened constantly during his long
residence in the country. A day or two after his
arrival he dined with Lafayette, who showed him
a draft of the famous declaration of rights. " I
gave him my opinions," Mr. Morris wrote in his
diary, "and suggested several amendments tend-
ing to soften the high-colored expressions of free-

dom. It is not by sounding words that revolutions
are produced." A few weeks later we find him
writing to Washington in the same strain, his
sense of humor thoroughly aroused by the queer
antics of the enthusiastic amateurs in government-
making who then swarmed and talked everywhere
in Paris. "Everything," he says, "is *à l'Anglais*,
and a desire to imitate the English prevails alike in
the cut of a coat and the form of a constitution."

Before a month had expired Mr. Morris had
become a social success, thanks to his wit, ability,
and engaging manners. Every day brought an
invitation to the *salon* of some fashionable woman,
or to the dinner table of some statesman or philosopher. Full accounts, apparently, are given in the
diary of all these entertainments, but Mr. Sparks
seems to have thought them below the dignity of
history, for he has favored us with only one or two
extracts, and as a rule has confined his selections
to politics.[1] The observations on public affairs
are penetrating and valuable in the highest degree,
but the descriptions of the social life, of men and
women of the world, of the more private side of
daily life, are most charming and interesting. The
characteristic vein of subdued satire, the keenness
of observation, the effective style of these passages, are extremely attractive, and they cannot
but cause the greatest regret that we should not
have them entire. There is no other journal, diary,
or correspondence of that period left by any of

[1] This has been largely remedied in the edition of the
diary published by Miss Morris.

our public men which at all compares with this in its amusing, light, and humorous touch. From the slender selections of Mr. Sparks let us take this : —

"March 3d. Monsieur le Comte de Nenni does me the honor of a visit, and detains me till three o'clock. I then set off in great haste to dine with the Comtesse de B., on an invitation of a week's standing. Arrive at about a quarter past three, and find in the drawing-room some dirty linen and no fire. While a waiting-woman takes away one, a valet lights up the other. Three small sticks in a deep bed of ashes give no great expectation of heat. By the smoke, however, all doubts are removed respecting the existence of fire. To expel the smoke a window is opened, and, the day being cold, I have the benefit of as fresh air as can reasonably be expected in so large a city.

"Towards four o'clock the guests begin to assemble, and I begin to expect that, as Madame is a poetess, I shall have the honor to dine with that exalted part of the species who devote themselves to the Muses. In effect, the gentlemen begin to compliment their respective works, and as regular hours cannot be expected in a house where the mistress is occupied more with the intellectual than the material world, I have a delightful prospect of a continuance of the scene. Towards five Madame steps in to announce dinner, and the hungry poets advance to the charge. As they bring good appetites they have certainly reason to praise the feast, and I console myself in the persuasion that for this day, at least, I shall escape an indigestion.

A very narrow escape, **too,** for some rancid butter, of which the cook had been liberal, puts me in bodily fear. **If the** repast is not abundant, we have at least the consolation that there is no lack **of** conversation. **Not** being perfectly master **of the language, most of the jests escaped me. As for the rest of the company, each** being employed either in **saying a good thing or in studying one** to say, **it is no wonder if he cannot find time to** applaud **that of** his neighbor. **They all** agree **that** we live in an age alike deficient in justice **and** in taste. Each finds in the fate of his own works numerous instances to justify this assertion. They **tell** me, to my great surprise, that the public **now** condemn **theatrical** compositions **before they have heard the first recital. And to remove my** doubts **the Countess is so kind as to assure me** that **this rash decision has been made on one of her own pieces. In pitying modern degeneracy we rise from the table.''**

The statement **as to the condemnation of theatrical** works smacks **of the soil. In the words '' to** my great **surprise '' we catch the** peculiar **vein of** American humor **which delights in a solemn ap-**pearance **of** ignorant **and innocent belief in some** preposterous assertion. **It is close kin to the broader form** exemplified by **Mark Twain weeping at the grave of** Adam, which **the ''Saturday Re-view ''** declared **was a ridiculous affectation of sen-timent.**

March **25th Mr. Morris was at the** house **of his** old and **true** friend **of the Revolution, Madame de**

Chastellux. There he met the Duchess of Orleans, and formed a friendship which was to prove very warm, very faithful, and of great service to the Duchess and her son, the citizen king of the future. Two days later he went to dine with the Neckers in company with his friend the Maréchal de Castries. Here too he began a lifelong friendship with both his host and the daughter of the house, Madame de Staël, which was kept up with real affection on all sides until death ended it. His first impressions of M. Necker are worth quoting for their shrewd correctness: "A little before dinner, Monsieur enters. He has the look and manner of the counting-house, and, being dressed in embroidered velvet, he contrasts strongly with his habiliments. His bow, his address, say, 'I am the man.' Our company is one half Academicians. The Duchess of Biron, formerly Lauzun, is one. I observe that M. Necker seems occupied by ideas which rather distress him. He cannot, I think, stay in office half an hour unless the nation insist on keeping him there. He is now much harassed, and Madame receives continally *mémoires* from different people; so that she seems as much occupied as he is. If he is really a very great man I am deceived; and yet this is a rash judgment. If he is not a laborious man I am also deceived."

While he was thus watching and weighing the men and women whose brilliant society he so much enjoyed, he was also studying with deep attention the momentous political development going on about him. May 4th, the day before the opening

of the States-General, he witnessed the procession
at Versailles. The Queen was received with hostile silence, and Mr. Morris wrote most characteris-
tically, "I cannot help feeling the mortification
which the poor Queen meets with, for I see only
the woman, and it seems unmanly to treat a woman
with unkindness." He was present at the opening
of the States-General, and has left a very striking
and picturesque description of that great event, unfortunately too long for quotation. He followed
the operations of that famous body with close scru-
tiny, and found little in their doings to encourage
him as to the prospects of France. We catch a
glimpse here of another famous American, who was
equally interested in the fortunes of the French
people, but who looked upon the advancing revolution with feelings and opinions very different from
those of Mr. Morris.

"June 3d. Go to Mr. Jefferson's. Some political conversation. He seems to be out of hope of
anything being done to purpose by the States-General. This comes from having sanguine expecta-
tions of a downright republican form of government. The literary people here, observing the
abuses of their monarchical form, imagine that
everything must go better in proportion as it re-
cedes from the present establishments, and in their
closets they make men exactly suited to their systems ; but unluckily they are such men as exist nowhere else, and least of all in France."

He had still other occupations, as appears by the
next entry, with its jest at his own expense : —

" June 5th. Go to M. Houdon's. He has been waiting for me a long time. I stand for his statue of General Washington, being the humble employment of a manikin. This is literally taking the advice of St. Paul to be all things to all men."

June 6th, he supped with Madame **Flahaut**, where he met a certain very celebrated person, whom he gauged with his usual penetrating accuracy : " The Bishop of Autun, who is one of our company, and an intimate friend of Madame Flahaut, appears to me a sly, cool, cunning, ambitious, and malicious man. I know not why conclusions so disadvantageous to him are formed in my mind ; but so it is, and I cannot help it." This quick judgment which Mr. Morris here sets down when Talleyrand was still comparatively unknown does not differ very widely from that of posterity half a century after the death of that eminent statesman and divine. It is one of many instances of a foresight and insight amounting almost to a gift of prophecy which made Mr. Morris's political predictions so wonderful in their correctness.

Let us take a few more extracts from the diary : —

" June 23d. At dinner I sit next to M. de Lafayette, who tells me that I injure the cause, for that my sentiments are continually quoted against the good party. I seize this opportunity to tell him that I am opposed to the democracy from regard to liberty ; that I see they are going headlong to destruction, and would fain stop them if I could ; that their views respecting this nation are totally

inconsistent with the materials of which it is composed ; and that the worst thing which could happen would be to grant their wishes. **He** tells me
that he is sensible that his party are **mad**, and tells
them so, but is not the less determined to **die with
them.** **I** tell him that I think it would **be quite as
well to bring them to their senses and live with**
them."

It is plain that he concealed nothing **from La-**
fayette, no **matter** how distasteful **his** advice might
prove. He wrote in **the same way to** Washington,
ten days later : —

" Our American example has done them good,
but, like all novelties, liberty runs away with their
discretion, if they **have any.** They want an American constitution, **with** the exception of a King instead of a President, **without** reflecting that they
have not American citizens to support that constitution." When he penned **this sentence the** first
storm was **just about to burst.** July 14th, the day
of the taking of **the** Bastile, **after describing that**
event and the manner **in which he heard of it, Mr.**
Morris writes, with a turn at the **end** which is **very**
characteristic, " Yesterday **it was the** fashion **at**
Versailles not to believe that there were **any dis-**
turbances **at** Paris. I presume **that** this day's
transaction will induce a conviction that all is **not**
perfectly quiet." After the fall of the Bastile
there was a lull, **and the** attempts at constitution-
making and reform **went on** again after a **fashion.**

September 26th, **Mr.** Morris **was at** the National
Assembly, whither, **indeed, he went frequently, and**

after listening to the report of the Minister of
Finance he remarked, " At the close, however, of
the report there is a feebleness which they are not,
perhaps, fully aware of, or perhaps it was unavoid-
able. They appeal to patriotism for aid ; but they
should in money matters apply only to interest.
They should never acknowledge such want of resource as to render the aid of patriotism necessary." So annoyed and troubled was he by the
errors which he saw committed that, as events hur-
ried rapidly forward, he strove, of course in vain,
to mend matters by appealing to his intimate
friends in behalf of wiser measures.

October 16th, he wrote to Lafayette an admirable letter of counsel and advice. He said that the
constitution would not work, and that the National
Assembly would soon fall into contempt. Under
these circumstances, the only thing to be done was
to strengthen the executive, and he urged Lafayette
to see that good and able men go into the council,
but advised Lafayette himself to remain outside.
The reasons for this advice are then set forth with
great vigor and shrewdness. One cannot help
thinking, as one reads these wise but futile words,
what a pity it was that among the French statesmen there were not a few like Morris. Much
might have been saved if there had been, but nothing is so empty as the " ifs " of history. There
were no such men in France, for there had been
no chance for centuries to breed them, or even to
make them possible.

Mr. Morris was now called away by public duties of his own. He was requested by Washington to go to England as a secret agent of our government, and endeavor to reopen diplomatic relations and settle various outstanding and threatening differences with that country. To London he accordingly went in February, 1790, and there he spent seven or eight months in fruitless conversations with the Duke of Leeds and Mr. Pitt about western posts, the fulfillment of treaties, the compensation for negroes, British debts, and impressment. On the last subject he said, with a concise wit which ought to have made the saying more famous than it is, " I believe, my lord, that this is the only instance in which we are not treated as aliens." Whether this keen-edged remark penetrated the heavy mind of the noble duke to whom it was addressed does not appear. At all events, the mission was a failure. English ministers, with that sagacity which has characterized them in dealing with the United States, were determined to injure us so far as they could, and to make us enemies instead of friends, if it were possible to do so, — a policy which has borne lasting fruit, and which England does not now delight in quite so much as of yore.

It is pretty obvious that Mr. Morris was not to their taste, despite his wit and good manners. He was a man of perfect courage and patriotism, and could be neither bullied nor cajoled. His brother, Staats Long Morris, was a general in the British army and the husband of the Duchess of Gordon, — a fact which implied respectability to the English mind, and made it difficult for them to snub a person who, according to their notions, was so well connected. Worst of all, he was a man of great ability and wide information, intellectually superior to any minister he met, except Mr. Pitt, and therefore he was an awkward person to trample on. Stories were set afloat to injure him, and were so far successful that they gave him much trouble at home. He was charged with consorting with Fox and the opposition, which was not true, and with revealing his purposes to Luzerne, the French minister, which was true, and sprang from Mr. Morris's sentiment of gratitude to France, ill rewarded, and in great measure cured, by Luzerne's betrayal of his confidence. He found time, however, in the midst of his vain efforts, to observe his English friends, and the following extract from a letter to Washington shows that the ludicrous side in the lives of the various distinguished personages whom he met did not escape him.

On September 18, 1790, he wrote of Pitt: "Observe that he is rather the Queen's man than the King's, and that since his majesty's illness she has been of great consequence. This depends in part on a medical reason. To prevent the relapse of persons who have been mad they must be kept in constant awe of somebody; and it is said that the physician of the King gave the matter in charge to his royal consort, who performs that, like every other part of her conjugal duty, with singular zeal and perseverance."

Fruitless wranglings and disobliging treatment,

although they could not disturb his good-humor,
nevertheless tired him sadly, and he turned his
eyes ever more wistfully to the exciting scenes in
France. He showed this in a letter to a friend in
Paris, in which, too, he made one of his many correct predictions, and also revealed his knowledge
of his own failing in the direction of a dangerous
frankness.

"A cautious man," he says, "should therefore
give only sibylline predictions, if indeed he should
hazard any. But I am not a cautious man. I
therefore give it as my opinion that they will issue
the paper currency, and substitute thereby depre-
ciation in the place of bankruptcy, or, rather, sus-
pension."

Soon after he departed for the Continent, made
a brief tour in Germany, and in November reached
Paris again. He went at once to one of his old
haunts, the club, and there met his friend De
Moustier, who was engaged in making a constitution, and was, "as usual, on the high ropes of
royal prerogative." He soon saw that things were
going to pieces very rapidly, and after several
visits finally got an opportunity to tell Lafayette
so, and to renew his former advice to rally about
the throne and try to gain some stability; express-
ing at the same time unbounded contempt for "the
thing called a constitution." He also urged the
restoration of the nobility, at which poor Lafayette
flinched, and said he would like two chambers, as
in America. "I tell him that an American constitution will not do for this country; that every

country must have a constitution suited to its circumstances, and the state of France requires a higher-toned government than that of England." All this was very true but very unpalatable, especially to Lafayette, and the result was that he became rather cool to his frank adviser. Yet the old friendship really remained as warm as ever, and when Lafayette became a prisoner no one worked harder for his liberation than Mr. Morris.

Although the tremendous events in the midst of which he was now plunged absorbed his thoughts, we still get here and there glimpses of the gay society in which he found himself, and which was soon to be extinguished in the dark torrent of revolution.

January 19, 1791, he wrote : " Visit Madame de Chastellux, and go with her to dine with the Duchess of Orleans. Her royal highness is ruined ; that is, she is reduced from 450,000 to 200,000 livres per annum. She tells me that she cannot give any good dinners ; but if I will come and fast with her, she will be glad to see me."

January 25th, he dined with Madame de Staël, and heard the Abbé Sieyès " descant with much self-sufficiency on government." Four days later he went out to Choisy with Madame de Chastellux and dined with Marmontel, who seemed to his guest " to think soundly," a compliment paid by Mr. Morris to but few of his French friends. There is something very striking and most interesting in these little pictures of daily existence, which went on much as usual, although the roar of revolution was sounding in men's ears. Philosophers speculated and fine ladies jested, even if the world was in convulsion; and so they continued to do until it was all drowned in the Terror, from which arose, after brief interval, another society, as light-hearted and brilliant, if not so well born, as its predecessor.

We can mark, however, the tremendous changes in progress around him in the extracts from the diary. The social pictures grow fewer, the tone is graver, there are more interviews with states-men and fewer chats with ladies of rank, while the reflections concern the welfare of state and na-tion rather than the foibles or graces of men and women. April 4th came the funeral of Mirabeau, with some observations in the diary which are elo-quent and striking; and there were other and still weightier matters then pressing upon his mind. August 26th he noted in his diary, " Dine with Madame de Staël, who requests me to show her the mémoire I have prepared for the King." The next day he wrote, " Dine with M. de Montmorin. After dinner retire into his closet and read to him the plan I have prepared of a discourse for the King. He is startled at it. Says it is too forci-ble; that the temper of the people will not bear it." Mr. Morris's talents and the force of his argu-ments on the state of public affairs had attracted general attention, and in their agony of doubt court and ministry turned to him for aid. The result was the draft for a royal speech, which the King liked but was prevented by his ministers from using, a mémoire on the state of France, notes for a constitution, and some other similar papers which are given by Mr. Sparks. These documents are very able and bold. Whether Mr. Morris's policy, if pursued, would have had any effect may well be doubted, but there can be no question that it was the sanest, most vigorous, and best defined of the multitude offered to poor, hesitating Louis, and its adoption could certainly have done no harm. In the midst of these disinterested and somewhat perilous pursuits we find him writing to Robert Morris (October 10, 1791), and describing a scene at the theatre when the people cheered the King and Queen.

"Now, my dear friend," he adds, "this is the very same people who, when the King was brought back from his excursion, whipped a democratical duchess of my acquaintance because they heard only the last part of what she said, which was, ' Il ne faut pas dire, Vive le Roi.' She had the good sense to desire the gentleman who was with her to leave her. Whipping is, you know, an operation which a lady would rather undergo among strangers than before her acquaintance."

Mr. Morris's sympathy for the King and Queen led him on further than he anticipated. Indeed, his attitude as an adviser of the ministry caused outbreaks against him on the part of the opposition. De Warville said in his newspaper that Morris, on one of his periodical visits to England upon business, was sent to thwart Talleyrand, — an accusation which Mr. Morris met with a public denial. His doings, however, were not fortunate, in view of the responsibility about to be placed upon him ; for while he was away on this very visit to England, in the early months of 1792, he received the news of his appointment as minister to France.

Morris was not without enemies. At home, his contempt and dislike for the methods of the French Revolution were only too well known, and his confirmation was strongly opposed in the Senate. His good friend the President with much delicacy explained to him the ground of the opposition, and in this way pointed out to Morris the failings which threatened his success. The idea of your political adversaries, Washington said, is " that the promptitude with which your lively and brilliant imagination displays itself allows too little time for deliberation and correction, and is the primary cause of those sallies which too often offend, and of that ridicule of character which begets enmity not easy to be forgotten, but which might easily be avoided if it were under the control of more caution and prudence." If it had been known in America just how deeply Mr. Morris had plunged into French politics, it may be doubted whether Washington even would have nominated him as minister. As it turned out, no better choice could have been made, yet at the moment Mr. Morris was involved in affairs which no foreign minister ought even to have known. He probably felt that his efforts to save order and government by means of the monarchy were hopeless, but they had drawn him on into the much more dangerous path of personal sympathy for the King and Queen, and thence into attempts to, at least, preserve their lives. The King was unable to adopt Mr. Morris's views in his public utterances, but on his advice confided in M. de Monciel, one of his ministers, and this gentleman and Mr. Morris arranged an elaborate yet practicable scheme for the escape of the royal family. After a short time the King sent Mr. Morris 547,000 livres to carry out the plan, and wished also to make him the depositary of his papers. Mr. Morris accepted the first trust, and declined the latter. The large sum of money seems to indicate the King's preference for the plan of Mr. Morris, in whom he had great confidence, yet there were half a dozen other schemes on foot at the same time. De Molleville had one ; Mr. Crawford, sent over by the British government, had another ; Marie Antoinétte's Swedish friend, Count Fersen, had a third ; and there were probably many more. One plan interfered with another. That of Morris and Monciel was ripe for execution, and still the King doubted and delayed. While he was hesitating, the 10th of August came, the Swiss guard was massacred, and all was over.

An American gentleman was present at the Tuileries on that memorable day, and went thence to the house of the minister of the United States. On entering he found Mr. Morris surrounded by the old Count d'Estaing and many other persons of distinction, who had fought side by side with us in our war for independence. Silence reigned, interrupted only by the weeping of the women and children. As the visitor was about to retire, Mr. Morris took him aside, and said, " I have no doubt, sir, but there are persons on the watch, who would find fault with my conduct as minister in receiving and protecting these people ; but I call on you to witness the declaration which I now make, and that is, that they were not invited to my house, but came of their own accord.   Whether my house will be a protection to them, or to me, God only knows, but I will not turn them out of it, let what will happen to me.   You see, sir, they are all persons to whom our country is more or less indebted, and it would be inhuman to force them into the hands of these assassins, had they no such claim upon me."   Whatever the faults of Mr. Morris, or whatever criticism may be made upon him, no American even now can read these words, uttered at such a moment, without feeling his pulse beat quicker, and without rejoicing that a man of such high and generous spirit so fitly represented his country in an hour of trial and peril.

To suppose, however, because Mr. Morris had the sympathy of a gallant man for the King and Queen in their danger and distress, and also profound distrust and contempt as an able and practical statesman for the follies and madness of those who were trying to carry on the French Revolution, that he therefore was a lover of royalty and aristocracy and titles would be a great injustice.   How far removed he really was from such weak prejudices is shown by an incident many years later.   At Vienna, where he had a discussion with some of the *émigrés* and

with some scions of Austrian nobility in regard to
Lafayette, these precious individuals abused the
fallen and imprisoned leader ferociously, and Mr.
Morris of course came to his defense. His com-
mentary shows how much he despised the people
who might have saved France, and failed. "Indeed, the conversation of these gentlemen, who
have the virtue and good fortune of their grand-
fathers to recommend them, leads me almost to forget the crimes of the French Revolution ; and often
the unforgiving temper and sanguinary wishes
which they exhibit make me almost believe that the
assertion of their enemies is true, namely, that it is
success alone which has determined on whose side
should be crimes and on whose the misery."

In the same vein and about the same time he
said of the illustrious personage who afterwards
became Louis XVIII. that " in his opinion he had
nothing to do but to try to get shot, thereby redeeming by valor the foregone follies of his conduct." He was sorry for the King and Queen, he
disliked and distrusted utterly the methods of the
Revolution, but he despised the French royalty
and nobility, for " they turned like cravens, and
fled."

The two years which followed his appointment
as minister make one of the most brilliant chapters
in the diplomatic history of the United States. On
the day he left Paris, after having turned everything over to his successor, Mr. Monroe, Mr. Morris
wrote in his diary (October 12, 1794), " I have the
consolation to have made no sacrifice either of per-

sonal or national dignity, and I believe I should
have obtained everything if the American government had refused to recall me." [1]

This brief statement is as true as it is moderate.
No foreign minister ever faced such difficulties and
dangers as Mr. Morris did at this time, for the simple reason that there has been in modern times but
one Reign of Terror, and Mr. Morris was the only
representative of a foreign government who did not
ask for his passports and withdraw. He not only
remained at his post, but he handled the affair of
our debt most admirably, doing all that either law
or honor demanded to accelerate our payments, but
firmly declining to go farther, or to be imposed
upon in any way. He carried on a continual battle with the decrees militating against our com-
merce, met every difficulty that arose at the thresh-
old, protested against every outrage on our rights,
and was on the point of getting reparation when
the French government obtained his recall. If
these duties had been performed in ordinary times
they would have been sufficiently difficult, but to
deal with any diplomatic questions in the hurly-
burly of the French Revolution seems an almost
impossible feat. Mr. Morris, on account of his
well-known views, was not liked by the successive
ministries or committees, each of whom was more
extreme and violent than its predecessor. To
oppose them was about as safe as playing with a

---

[1] Our government had demanded the recall of Genet, and
the French rulers took advantage of this to ask in turn for
the recall of Morris, whom they both feared and disliked.

hungry tiger, but our minister never flinched by a hair's breadth. His house was searched more than once, he was arrested in the street because he did not have his card of citizenship, and his death or murder was at one time currently reported in Europe and America. His life was, in truth, in constant danger. When all other foreign ministers departed he stayed, an example worthily followed by another American minister when France was last beset with " malice domestic and foreign levy." When subjected to these various outrages he never failed to take a high tone, demand his passport, and obtain a more or less surly apology. So he held out, doing his duty and protecting his countrymen and his country's interests. He was, in fact, just the man for the place and time. A sympathizer like Monroe at that period would have been ensnared and made a tool of, and would have thus involved us in all the network of French complications, as indeed he afterwards succeeded in doing to a certain extent. Almost any other man of Morris's own party would have been driven from the country by holding a too rigid and defiant attitude. Morris, however, while too strongly opposed to the Revolution to be beguiled, by his utter fearlessness and ready wit, combined with a certain dash and gallantry, was carried through triumphantly. The diary became too dangerous, and was stopped for the time ; but before this occurred there are a few entries and some extracts from letters which must be quoted, to show how wonderfully he penetrated the conditions of the struggle, and how clearly he understood its true character. On May 14, 1792, he wrote to Washington : —

" You know that I do, from the bottom of my heart, wish well to this country, and will therefore easily judge what I have felt in seeing them long since in the high road to despotism."

And again, in June, he wrote : —

" It is notorious that the great mass of the French nation is less solicitous to preserve the present order of things than to prevent the return of the ancient oppressions, and of course would more readily submit to a pure despotism than to that kind of monarchy whose only limits were found in those noble legal and clerical corps by which the people were alternately oppressed and insulted."

Here is the true view of the French Revolution : that it was a struggle not for political theories, but for equality before the law, for the abolition of privileges, and for good government. Morris was almost if not quite alone, at that time, in this opinion, and it has been reserved to the most recent modern investigation to bring out and insist upon this all-important truth.

July 2d he wrote in his diary, " Monciel and Bremond call on me. The French, says Monciel, are, I am afraid, too rotten for a free government. I tell him that the experiment may, nevertheless, be tried, and despotism still remain as a last resort."

August 22d he wrote to Jefferson of Lafayette's flight : " Thus his circle is completed. He has spent his fortune on a revolution, and is now crushed by the wheel which he put in motion. He lasted longer than I expected."

October 18, 1793, he wrote to Washington: " But whatever may be the lot of France in remote futurity, and putting aside the military events, it seems evident that she must soon be governed by a single despot. Whether she will pass to that point through the medium of a triumvirate or other small body of men seems as yet undetermined. I think it most probable that she will."

If we consider that the Directory did not come until two years later, the consulate or triumvirate four years after that, and then in the process of evolution the Empire and the single despot in 1804, it must be admitted that this is an extraordinary example of political foresight. Morris saw that a despotism existed ; in common with many others he perceived that it would probably be concentrated in a single individual ; but who else in 1793 announced that the single despot would come in the precise manner in which it actually happened ? He made many other predictions, and was rarely wrong. Indeed, his sagacity in this way was quite noted among his friends, but there is space to mention only one other instance. Many years afterward, when watching from across the Atlantic with intense interest the Russian campaign, he predicted that Napoleon would begin his retreat from Moscow on October 21st. On October 19th the retreat actually began. These things were of course not due to mere

chance; and to M. Necker (May 22, 1798), who
had recalled one of his predictions since become
true, Mr. Morris gives undoubtedly the secret of
his remarkable foresight. "It is not," he says,
"difficult to prophesy in such a case. If we are
to judge of the conduct of a man in a given situation, it would be hazardous to pronounce upon it,
since the character of each individual is governed
by the peculiarity of his mind and the impression
made upon him by the circumstances in which he
is placed. But where the mass is concerned we
have but to observe the instinct of the animal,
and we shall not be deceived." In addition to this
wise doctrine he was also governed by a theory
which guided him through all his public life, and
largely explains his success. He said in a letter
to Carmichael : —

"The true object of a great statesman is to give
to any particular nation the kind of laws which is
suitable to them, and the best constitution which
they are capable of." No better rule was ever
laid down, and if it were more observed men would
make fewer disastrous failures in government and
constitutions.

After leaving France, Mr. Morris traveled for
six years on the Continent and in England, studying men and manners, enjoying society, and making
everywhere firm friends among the most distinguished men and women of the time. At last in
1799 he returned to America, and as he supposed
to private life and the practice of his profession.
He was elected, however, almost at once Senator

from New York, and reëntered public life just as the Federalist party, to which he belonged, was driven from power, never to return.

In the dangerous crisis which arose from the equality of votes received by Jefferson and Burr Mr. Morris took the only sound view, that it was right to have Jefferson chosen. He said in his driest way : —

"Not meaning to enter into intrigues, I have merely expressed the opinion that, since it was evidently the intention of our fellow-citizens to make Mr. Jefferson their President, it seems proper to fulfill that intention."

A little later he wrote to Hamilton : "I have more at the request of others than from my own mere motion suggested certain considerations not quite unworthy of attention ; but it is dangerous to be impartial in politics. You who are temperate in drinking have perhaps noticed the awkward situation of a man who continues sober after the company are drunk."

Again he wrote to Livingston : "I greatly disapproved, and openly disapproved, the attempt to choose Mr. Burr. Many of my friends thought differently. I saw they would be disappointed, and therefore looked on with perfect composure. Indeed, my dear friend, this farce of life contains nothing which should put us out of humor."

Despite his philosophy, however, he made a most eloquent and desperate resistance to the repeal of the judiciary act, which he always considered little less than a death-blow to the Constitution. He could be impartial at times, and he supported the acquisition of Louisiana, but at heart he was a strong partisan. We can see this in what he said of Jefferson.

"It is the fashion," he wrote in 1803, "with those discontented creatures called Federalists, to say that our President is not a Christian ; yet they must acknowledge that, in true Christian meekness, when smitten on one cheek he turns the other, and by his late appointment of Monroe has taken especial care that a stone which the builders rejected should become the first of the corner. These are his *works* ; and for his *faith*, it is not as a grain of mustard, but the full size of a pumpkin, so that while men of mustard-seed faith can only move mountains, he finds no difficulty in swallowing them. He believes, for instance, in the perfectibility of man, the wisdom of mobs, and moderation of Jacobins. He believes in payment of debts by diminution of revenue, in defense of territory by reduction of armies, and in vindication of rights by the appointment of ambassadors."

Again he wrote to Dayton : " That our administration is too feeble is, I believe, too true. What you say of their chief is curious. When he told you we have the choice of enemies, he stated a fact applicable at all times to all countries, since any blundering blockhead can make a war; but when he acknowledged that we have not a choice of friends, he pronounced the surest satire on himself, since this misfortune can only be attributed to a series of false and foolish measures."

Strong and even extreme as he was in his Federalism, he nevertheless was not despondent, like
so many of his party friends, and declined to despair of the future. "There is always," he said in a
letter written in 1803, "a counter-current in human
affairs, which opposes alike both good and evil.
Thus the good we hope is seldom obtained, and
the evil we fear is rarely realized. . . . Like the
forked, featherless bipeds which have preceded
them, our posterity will be shaken into the political form which shall be most suitable to their physi-
cal and moral state. They will be born, procreate,
and die, like the rest of creation, while here and
there some accomplished scoundrels, *rari nantes
in gurgite vasto*, will give their names to periods
of history."

He seems to have sighed but little for the delights of Europe, where he had passed so many
years. To his friend Parish, who urged him to
come to England, he wrote in 1807 : —

" Recollect that a tedious morning, a great dinner, a boozy afternoon, and dull evening make the
sum total of English life. It is admirable for the
young men who shoot, hunt, drink ; but for us !
How are we to dispose of ourselves ? No. Were
I to give you a rendezvous in Europe, it should
be on the Continent."

He traveled extensively, however, in his own
country, and not content with the exercise of his
profession, gave his best thought and work to
schemes of public improvement. As early as 1777
Mr. Morris had set forth the idea of connecting

the great lakes with the Hudson. This project he never forgot, and after his return he renewed his efforts, and devoted the last years of his life and all his eloquence before the legislature to its promotion.

Thus engaged, his life flowed peacefully along. He married in 1809, most happily, and not long afterwards, in a letter to his friend Madame de Damas, he gives us a glimpse of himself and his home life that displays admirably the happy disposition, cheerful philosophy, and keen intellect which made their possessor so successful and so contented. " My health," he wrote, " is excellent, saving a little of the gout which at this moment annoys me. I can walk three leagues, if the weather be pleasant and the road not rough. My employment is to labor for myself a little, for others more ; to receive much company, and forget half those who come. I think of public affairs a little, play a little, read a little, and sleep a good deal. With good air, a good cook, fine water and wine, a good constitution and a clear conscience, I descend towards the grave full of gratitude to the Giver of all good."

There is nothing to add but the inevitable statement of the end. He died after a brief illness, in 1816, without suffering and cheerful to the last.

The man who made the final draft of the Constitution of the United States, and who first suggested the Erie Canal, needs no other monuments. But his brilliant intellect and long and distinguished public career deserve to be well known. We have but to read his diaries and letters to appre-

ciate him at his true value both as statesman and
writer. There is only one other word to be said.
Among many fine qualities of heart and mind,
nothing does him more honor than his strong, un-
swerving patriotism and ardent belief in his country. This sketch cannot end more fitly than with
another prediction, made in 1801, which has not
only been fulfilled, but which shows the spirit
which animated its author throughout his life : —

" The proudest empire in Europe is but a bauble
compared to what America *will* be, *must* be, in the
course of two centuries, perhaps of one ! If, with
a calm retrospect to the progress made within
forty years, we stand on the firm ground of calcu-
lation, warranted by experience, and look forward
to the end of a similar period, imagination shrinks
from the magnitude of rational deduction."

WHY PATRONAGE IN OFFICES IS UN-AMERICAN.[1]

CIVIL Service Reform has had a stormy existence of twenty-three years. It has moved along amid the abuse of foes, who have sneered at its advocates, and the loud praise of friends, who have showered much indiscriminate invective on all its enemies, real and supposed. Like other causes at bottom righteous it has marched forward, slowly and painfully, yet still forward. Nevertheless in all the noise and dust and shouting the precise thing wanted occasionally becomes dim, the line of march is sometimes lost, and the results reached are often hidden from sight. Any one who watches the course of a reform like this and sees it struggling among confusions born of much violent argument and talking hither and thither, for and against, is strongly tempted to cry out with Carlyle: "O shrieking beloved brother blockheads of mankind! let us close those wide mouths of ours; let us cease shrieking and begin considering." In the language of the shop, let us stop and take stock, that we may know the real state of the case, what we have got, what we want, and how we are to get that which is still lacking. As Mr. Webster said on a celebrated occasion, after tossing on the

[1] Reprinted from *The Century* for October, 1890.

waves of debate it is well to take our latitude and see how far we have been driven from the true course.

This is especially desirable in this instance, for no movement has ever suffered more through needless misstatement at the hands of both friends and foes than this effort to obtain better methods of administration in the public service. The very name itself is misleading, for the real intent of the movement is not to reform the civil service, but to change the mode by which its places are filled. The true purpose of civil service reform is to take the routine offices of the government which are not political out of politics, where they ought never to have been, and to substitute for personal patronage in appointments some system which shall be impersonal and disinterested. The improvement of the service itself is a secondary object, for the civil service of the United States has been as a rule very good, and a movement therefore, which by its title demanded only a reform of the service, and which at the outset was chiefly urged on that ground, started on false premises. This misfortune in naming is undoubtedly the chief reason that the movement for so long a time appealed so little to the American people, who are extremely practical, and who are inclined to resent anything which seems to them merely a fanciful effort to redress an unreal or trivial grievance. It is possible that no better name could have been devised. It is quite certain that it will not now be changed, and it is also certain that its real meaning is coming to be rightly understood.

The name, however, is the least of the difficulties. Both friend and foe seem to have conspired to pile up confusions about the movement in the form of argument and description. To begin with, there seems to be an absolute determination to misstate the case historically. The especial advocates of the reform have, as a rule, seen fit to take an arbitrary point in our history and declare that there and then what they call the spoils system was born. This theory coincides pleasantly with the belief not uncommon in certain circles that things political are much worse than they used to be once upon a time, and that we have fallen away sadly from the high standards of the fathers and founders of the Republic. These admirers of the past apparently consider that the only statesmen are dead statesmen, and that living public men are mere " politicians " — a word which has come to be, like the " spoils system," a term of art. In the good old days — exact date not given — the evils of modern public life, according to this doctrine, did not exist. Everybody who held office then was good and able, and was chosen or appointed solely from merit, while selfish politicians and mercenary lobbyists were unknown. In short, human nature then was something very different from what it is to-day.

This is not the place to deal with this particular nonsense, which springs either from ignorance or from falsification of the facts, not only of our own history, but of all history. The only thing that concerns us here is its application to the civil ser-

vice question. It appears to have passed into a
dogma that political patronage began with Andrew
Jackson, and that the proposed reform is simply
an effort to bring the civil service back to the pure
system of the early days of the Republic. The
exact truth is very different. The modern method
of selecting civil servants by examinations open to
all comers was as unknown in the early days of
the United States as the telegraph or the tele-
phone. When the government of the United
States was formed the only theory in regard to
appointments to office was the one then in vogue
everywhere, to the effect that they were matters
within the personal gift of the Chief Executive or
his representatives. Acting on this theory Washington appointed the officers of the government according to his good pleasure. That he was guided
by the highest and most disinterested motives, and
enlightened by the best information he could obtain
in making his selections, cannot be doubted. But
it is equally certain that he distributed the offices
solely as a matter of personal patronage ; that at
the start, with few exceptions, he appointed only
friends of the Constitution ; and that after the development of parties he appointed only Federalists,
laying down plainly in more than one letter the
doctrine that none but those who were friendly
to the government ought to receive the offices.
John Adams pursued the same general policy, and
his " midnight appointments " were as marked an
example of partisanship in filling offices as our
history can show.

Jefferson, after some delays and a few fine phrases, distributed a large percentage of the offices among his party adherents. No plainer statement of the spoils system was ever made than that laid down by Jefferson in the following letter to the New Haven remonstrants, — " If a due participation of office is a matter of right, how are vacancies to be obtained ? Those by death are few ; by resignation, none. Can any other mode than that of removal be proposed? This is a painful office, and I meet it as such." The rest of the letter, too long for quotation, is an argument on this theme, that offices are to be distributed according to politics, and removals made in order to get them. As Mr. Adams says with quiet sarcasm, in his " History of the United States," Jefferson did not go so " far as to assert that to the victors belong the spoils ; he contented himself with claiming that to the victors belonged half the spoils." The restriction was characteristic of the man, and less honest than Jackson's bold and frank determination to have everything ; but the principle in both cases was precisely the same. Moreover at this very time in some of the States, notably in New York and Pennsylvania, political patronage in government offices was carried out with a ferocious thoroughness unknown at the present day.

In the interval between Jefferson and Jackson political patronage subsided. Madison, long before his coming to the Presidency, had declared himself against removals without cause, which was also the view of the younger Adams, and probably of

Monroe as well. The real cause, however, of the small number of changes during this period lay deeper than the personal views and characters of the Presidents. The long continuance of one party in power, followed by the disappearance of the Federalists and the merging of all parties — nominally at least — in one, was the efficient and obvious reason for the small number of official changes under Madison, Monroe, and Adams. The system, however, remained at bottom entirely unchanged, and when Jackson came into power with a new set of followers and a new set of ideas, he merely put into active operation a practice which had slumbered for twenty years, but which had been the same from the beginning. Under Jackson the distribution of the offices for political purposes was extended and systematized, and the theory upon which it was done was thrown by Marcy into the now famous formula, "to the victors belong the spoils." Dating the spoils system from Jackson's time, therefore, is dating it from the declaration of the formula, which has no real connection with either its origin or its practice. Since Jackson's day, as the Government has grown, political patronage has grown, and spread, too, until it has assumed the enormous proportions with which the present generation is familiar. The effort to do away with it by an impersonal and disinterested machinery of appointment is a wholly modern idea, and is not in any sense a reversion to the early practice of the Republic.

The historical view of the ardent reformer, that

patronage in offices sprang **full fledged from** the brain of Andrew Jackson, seems purposeless in its inaccuracy except **so** far as it fits in with an *a priori* theory of modern political decadence. This cannot **be** said of the historical view of the enemy **of the** reform. Superficially more **exact than that of the** reformer, it is in reality **even** falser, **and at the same time** it is anything but purposeless, **for** its object **is to** discredit the **reform** in the eyes **of** the people. **The first historical** proposition of **the** opponent of the reform is that the patronage system has always existed in this country, and that the reformers seek to put something wholly new in its place. So far the opponent is perfectly correct; and he becomes misleading only when he advances to his second proposition, which is, that patronage **has not** only always been the system of dealing with **the** offices, **but** that **it is the American** system of civil service, **and that any** other scheme is open to the fatal objection of being un-American. This second proposition is wildly false. Patronage in office is no more a peculiarly **American** institution than **the** common **law or the** English language. **We** brought the patronage system with us **from** the Old World, as we brought **many** things, good and bad. Some of these importations were in their nature suited **to us and** our new **conditions, and** were **therefore** American. Others **were** wholly alien to our theory **and** practice in government, and therefore were un-American. To the **latter** class the patronage system peculiarly belongs.

After the **fall of the** feudal system, and the **rise,**

establishment, and consolidation of the monarchies of Europe the doctrine that the king was the fountain of honor received a great extension. It was perceived readily that as the king possessed the appointing power he had a vast opportunity in the public service and the public revenue for reward and punishment, for corruption and profit. In offices and sinecures, in pensions and contracts, the king could provide for his bastards and his favorites, his relations and his supporters. In the monarchies of Europe this was what patronage in offices meant, and it was dispensed with a profligacy which sowed seeds of revolution destined to bear a terrible harvest. In England patronage took another turn, as was to have been expected from her limited royal power and greater popular liberty. English statesmen soon discovered that public offices were the best and surest means to strengthen and maintain their political power, and that they had in them an almost unlimited fund for bribery. Sir Robert Walpole developed this system with his wonted ability, and made it one of the bulwarks of the unquestioned sway which he held so long. For more than a century after his time patronage prevailed everywhere in England. With a limited suffrage, rotten boroughs, and an aristocratic government it was a most powerful engine, and the personal and political corruption which it engendered is one of the commonplaces of history. When England had cast off the rotten boroughs and had enlarged her suffrage, when her government became democratic instead of aristocratic, the royal and aristocratic system of patronage broke down, and a system which accorded with modern civilization took its place.

In this country prior to the Revolution we had the patronage system of Sir Robert Walpole, own cousin to the foul and corrupt abuses of Louis XIV. and of the other monarchs of Europe. When the government of the United States was formed the wise men who framed the Constitution saw and rooted out one of the evils of patronage, although not perhaps the worst. They perceived very clearly that Parliament was controlled and corrupted in large measure by the bestowal of appointive offices upon its members, and in order to preserve the legislature of the United States from this danger they put a clause in the Constitution which made it impossible for the Executive to corrupt Congress by the appointment of its members to office. This makes it plain that the framers of the Constitution saw nothing sacredly American in official patronage. On the contrary, they detected in it in one direction a great peril, and in that direction they cut it up by the roots. They went no further, not from any particular faith in the system, but because they then knew no other way of filling offices than by the will and pleasure of the appointing power, and because the minor offices were so few that no man except an inspired prophet could have seen in them any danger. At all events the system thus modified endured unchanged and unassailed until within the last twenty years, when its rottenness became apparent from the vast increase of offices and consequent growth of patronage.

The system of patronage in offices, then, we have always had, but it is none the less a system born of despotisms and aristocracies, and it is the merest cant to call it American. It is a system of favoritism and nepotism, of political influence and personal intrigue. In a word it is as un-American as anything could well be, for a system by which Louis XIV. and his successors drained the life blood of the French people, and by which Sir Robert Walpole and his successor corrupted the British Parliament, has no proper place on American soil, and is utterly abhorrent to the ideas upon which the democratic government of the United States has been founded and built up. Whatever may be said for or against the substitute which is now in part established, it is at least grounded on the American idea of a fair field and no favor, and this of itself is sufficient to prove it superior to a system which is all favor and no field at all.

So much for the historical side of the question. Let us look now for a moment very briefly at the arguments for and against the reform.

In favor of the reform it is urged that by a mechanical system of examination, combined with permanency of tenure, a better quality of service will be secured. There can be no doubt that there is force in this argument. The chances are that you will get a better stenographer if you examine him on his ability to write short-hand rather than on his own political belief or that of his friends; and the same holds true of all branches of the government service. But the improvement to be obtained in this way is neither great enough nor sufficiently obvious to make it a controlling motive in the adoption of the reform. It is a sound but an altogether subsidiary argument.

A far stronger proposition in support of the reform is, that to stake on each presidential election the livelihood of all the thousands of people who hold government offices, and support themselves and their families by government work is to subject our institutions every four years to a grave and increasing peril, and to create a class of officeholders and mercenaries constantly increasing in numbers and seeking with the keen instinct of self-preservation to control the government. Such an enormous stake, involving the fortunes of so many people, bids fair to convert an election from a political contest into a struggle for existence on the part of large numbers of people, and such a struggle renders men desperate and ready for desperate acts. This argument of itself is enough to demonstrate the necessity of taking the civil service out of politics, and thus preventing the growth of a large class of people who regard politics not as a question between conflicting political principles, but as a mere battle for life and for money to live upon. The reality of this danger is great, and gives a force to the argument which no thoughtful man can question.

The last and most immediately practical argument in favor of the reform is that patronage places

upon Senators and Representatives, as well as upon
the chief executive officers, a burden which they
were never intended to sustain.   The immediate
result of this is that public interests are subordi-
nated to the private interests of the office-seekers.
Legislation suffers because those who ought to
legislate have their time occupied, their attention
distracted, and their minds fatigued by the in-
cessant demands of persons who seek places under
the government.   If the favorite theory of those
who oppose the reform, that the executive officers
in the various departments and bureaus are the
proper persons to select their own subordinates,
were carried into operation there would be little
need of the reform.   Department officers as a rule
desire to make successful administrations, and could
be trusted to select their subordinates wisely ; but
the fact is that the executive officers of the government do not, and under the patronage system
cannot, select their own subordinates with a view
solely to good administration.   As a matter of
fact their subordinates are selected for them by
Senators and Representatives, who are entirely ir-
responsible in regard to matters of administration,
and who are necessarily governed more or less by
personal and political interests which have no bearing on the execution of the public business.

It is perfectly true that a business man does not
select his clerks by a hard and fast competitive examination such as is applied now to a portion of
the government offices ; but on the other hand, a
business man who appointed his clerks on account

of their politics, or because some politician recommended them, would soon find his way into bankruptcy. The selection of subordinates in a private business is made practically by a competitive examination of the severest kind, managed by a watchful self-interest. The men who carry on the government and who recommend appointments have not the enlightened selfishness which business success demands to guide them. On the contrary, enlightened selfishness in their case makes personal advancement of the first importance, and the success of the business a very secondary matter. It is necessary, therefore, in dealing with the public service that we should substitute for the severe competitive examinations which are enforced by the conditions of business and commercial life some mechanical system which shall approach them as nearly as possible. The selection of clerks by competitive examination is a system which is no doubt imperfect, but it is infinitely better than that which it replaces. It has the cardinal merit of taking from the hands of Senators and Representatives a task for which they are not fitted and with which they should not be burdened, and of making the selection of subordinate officers disinterested and impersonal. Competitive examinations are not infallible, but they are better tests of fitness than the prejudices, friendships, and personal and political interests of men in public life. The exercise of patronage, moreover, is a source of weakness to every party and to every man who touches it, and it lowers the tone of public life, to the great injury of legislation and the public welfare. Yet until it is destroyed by law every public man must deal with it whether he wishes to or not, and if he refuses, his refusal is a mere shirking of duty.

Such are the principal, and, as it seems to me, conclusive, arguments in favor of maintaining and extending the reform of the civil service and the abolition of patronage. The arguments against it are for the most part mere appeals to prejudice. Such, for instance, is the reiterated statement that civil service reform is un-American, to which I have already referred and which is simply untrue. Patronage is un-American, and an impersonal system which offers a fair field and no favor is as distinctly democratic and American as anything well can be.

Another cry is that civil service reform is a foreign importation,— of Chinese origin, according to some authorities ; of English birth, according to others. Even were there meaning or truth in this, the answer would be easy. There is only one thing more contemptible than a feeble imitation of other people, and that is an equally feeble refusal to adopt something intrinsically good because somebody else has tried something like it and found it beneficial. We are hardly likely to abandon gunpowder or printing because the Chinese are said to have been the first inventors of both. Still less would it be a mark of high intelligence to revert to the Indian tongues because the language of the United States is that of England also.

Another objection of the opponents of the reform
which enjoys the lonely preëminence of deserving to
be called an argument, is that a permanent service
will lead to a civil pension list. If the one were in-
separable from the other this would be a very grave
objection, but a moment's reflection shows that
there is nothing in it. Men and women who enter
the government service are perfectly aware that
there is no retiring pension to be looked forward
to, and that if they decide to remain in the service
they must trust to their own exertions and their
own frugality, or to the formation with their asso-
ciates of an insurance fund, to make provision for
their old age, exactly as they would do if engaged
in any private business. If they are not willing to
do this the remedy is very simple, — they need not
enter the service.

The most common form of attack on civil service
reform, however, is to denounce it as a sham, and
by applying to it various contemptuous names to
make it ridiculous, and thus drive it out of existence. There is nothing easier in the world than
to sneer, and it is particularly easy to sneer at any
one who is trying to make things better. But the
sham in the civil service business does not lie with
those who are trying to make it a practical working
system, but with those who put it in their platforms,
who vote for it in their conventions and in Congress, and then go about assailing it as a hypocrit-
ical humbug. It is an inspiring sight to observe
the manly indignation expressed against civil service reform by its opponents on the ground that it

is a sham. To statesmen, politicians, and men in public life generally, nothing is so repulsive as humbug, for it is well known that they never indulge in it themselves, always voting and speech-making and resolving in exact accord with the hard, cold facts and never for effect. They would not object to civil service reform so much, they say, these hardy lovers of exact truth, were it not that it is a humbug. It is that feature which depresses and angers them. "The idea of discussing how clerks shall be appointed," says one, "when there are matters of real importance, great questions, before us! What can be more contemptible?" It does not seem to occur to them that it really is a mean thing to have appointments to office made grave political issues in every district and every State, and that they are so because they are kept in politics by patronage, which civil service reform aims to destroy. "Merit forsooth!" says another. "Clerks to be selected by merit! Bah! What a piece of pretentious humbug!" etc. This argument has the advantage of requiring no intellectual effort. Any one can make it by assuming a contemptuous tone and a sarcastic expression. At the same time it will be noted that merit governs these same people in selections for their own service. It is only in the service of the Government that they are so liberal to the unfortunate and the unworthy and so severe towards merit.

Yet another inquiry of the same type is that which asks with a sneer how men are ever to be encouraged to take part in politics if they are not to share in the rewards. It is wonderful that men should be found in the light of history to put forward such a staring absurdity as the proposition that in this day and generation you can carry on parties and win party victories by offices. Important elections turn on issues that affect the great mass of the people, not on the selfish interests of the few. In some large cities where a great mass of patronage, municipal, state, and national, is concentrated, the caucus or the convention, and sometimes the election, is decided by a compact body of officeholders, but with these exceptions offices are utterly ineffective. On the other hand, if patronage is of doubtful political advantage under the most propitious conditions, its disadvantages are glaring. To a party at large, as to an individual, it is, as an almost invariable rule, a source of weakness. The distribution of patronage is simply a distribution of factious quarrels throughout a State or a district, and no party and no man in the long run ever benefits by it.

I believe that I have now enumerated all the objections brought forward against the reform. It is rather a pitiful array, hardly to be dignified by the name of arguments; but after a somewhat protracted research and much patient listening I can find nothing else.

So far as the existing system of competitive examinations under the civil service goes, its opponents are more fertile in objections, but when these criticisms are fairly hunted down they generally turn out to be either without foundation or else extremely weak. In the first place, admitting all the imperfections that are charged, the opponents have nothing to offer in place of that which they propose to destroy, and they do not dare now to argue openly that a return to the system of patronage would be beneficial. They are fond of declaring that the examinations are scholastic and impracticable, but it is never possible to pin them down to a specific case. The commonest trick is to mix up the examinations, those for instance of assistant astronomers with those of clerks or letter carriers, and this confusion is the closest approach in my experience to a demonstration that the examinations are not practical. There was at the outset more force probably in this objection, but under the present commission such mistakes as there were in the character of the examinations have been largely if not entirely remedied.

Another point of criticism relates to the accumulation of names upon the eligible list, and a great deal of sympathy is poured out over the poor people whose names get on the lists, but who have no hope of being certified for appointment. The crowding of the eligible list could of course be avoided by simply raising the standard of examination ; but let us try it by the real test of a comparison with the old system. Out of every three eligibles on an average only one is appointed. Before the railway mail service went under the civil service law, in May, 1889, I had over sixty applicants for clerkships in that service. It was only possible for me or for any congressman in my

place to secure appointments for five. With few
exceptions, so far as I could judge from my own
inquiries, the applicants were all fairly eligible, and
therefore it appears that under the patronage system in this instance only one name in twelve reached
an appointment, instead of one in three as under
the reformed system. A wider and more conclusive example can be found in the diplomatic and
consular service. There are in that service, assuming that all are changed, between two and three
hundred places. As a matter of fact many are not
changed, and others are too trifling to excite com-
petition. Since the 4th of March, 1889, there have
been, as I am informed, 5,300 applications for posi-
tions in this service, and these applications are
practically confined to 119 places. In other words,
assuming that all the 119 are changed, one appli-
cant in fifty gets a place. It is not difficult to
imagine all the disappointment and heart-burning,
all the weary waiting and sickness from hope de-
ferred, caused by a system as monstrous as this,
which tempts and urges fifty men to seek an office,
with loss of time, money, and self-respect, only to
reject beyond recall forty-nine of them. It is easy
also to imagine the frightful waste of time caused
to the department officers, to the detriment of the
public business. The late Mr. Walker Blaine, of
the State Department, was reported in an interview
as declaring that a permanent consular service was
imperatively needed, and such is, I believe, the
opinion of all good judges.

I have no doubt that what happened in my own

experience, as well as in the case of the consular service, holds true as a general rule, and the explanation lies in the fact that patronage increases applications because it makes it seem as if it must be easy to get a place when it goes by favor and costs the giver nothing. The office-seekers forget that securing a place depends not on the method of selection, but on the number of places in proportion to the number of applications.

I have tried to state fairly the principal objections brought against the system now in actual operation. There are no others in my opinion worth consideration, and the recent attack upon the civil service commissioners, which was made because they enforced the law and not because they failed to do so, has not only signally vindicated Commissioners Roosevelt and Thompson and their policy, but has shown in a general way how remarkably well the new system is working.

There remains to be considered, however, one point in which both friends and foes of civil service reform are equally guilty, and which has tended more than anything else to obscure the real object of the reform and to retard its extension. This is the confusion of the patronage offices with those under the civil service law. With each succeeding Administration there is a loud cry raised that the spirit of the reform is not respected in regard to those offices which are confessedly filled by patronage. To remove without cause officers of a fixed tenure before the expiration of their term may be described as a violation of the true civil service prin-

ciple, but this is all that can be said with regard to
offices of the patronage class. Offices not in the
classified service will be emptied and filled by any
President, of any party, for personal or political motives, and whether it is done in one year or in four
is wholly unimportant. If the appointing officer
selects bad men he is justly censurable; but for the
mere fact of thus emptying and filling offices he
is not censurable, nor can any man administer a
patronage system in any other way. Civil service
reform is concerned with only two things, — the
administration of the civil service law, and its extension. If we go beyond this with talk about the
" spirit " of reform and applying the reform principle to offices not within the law, great confusion is
caused and an impression of insincerity is created,
which does and has done more to hinder the advance
of the genuine reform than anything else. In this
connection it may be said that it is much to be wished
that the charge of hypocrisy and pharisaism made
by the opponents of the reform had no foundation.
The reform itself in intent and in methods is honest,
simple, and devoid of sham, but there has been a
great deal of insincerity, as well as of the " better
than thou " tone, among those who have assumed a
particular guardianship over it. For example, to
pass over in dead silence the removal on political
grounds of a collector or a postmaster before his
time by the President of one party, and then to cry
out and get into a white heat with the President of
the opposite party for doing the same thing, is dishonest humbug of the worst kind. This attitude

has been common, and has done infinite harm
to the reform, because it has made the people
confuse some of the reformers with the reform itself, and believe that inasmuch as the former were
partisan and insincere the latter was a pretense and
a sham.

What, then, has actually been obtained, despite
attack and confusion, despite the mistakes of friends
and the assaults of foes? We have to-day over
thirty thousand of the most important and best paid
offices fairly out of politics and under the civil service law.[1] The system is so firmly established that

---

[1] Since this article was written President Harrison has extended the law to some seven hundred places in the Indian
service, where the change was sorely needed, and also to some
hundred and twenty places in the service of the Fish Commission. During the same period, also, Secretary Tracy has
put all the mechanics and laborers in the Navy Yards, some
six thousand five hundred men, under a purely civil service
system, based on that adopted in Boston for the city laborers.
Patronage has thus been entirely eliminated from the Navy
Yards, where for years it has been productive of the greatest
abuses. This is the greatest advance and extension of the
reform made since the passage of the law. The system is
rigidly competitive, and all that the most ardent civil service
reformer could desire. Unfortunately it rests only on a
department order, and an unfriendly Secretary could revoke
or evade it. The order should without delay be put into the
form of law, but although bills for that purpose have been
introduced, no action has thus far been taken. This change
in the employment of labor at the yards now has the support
of the labor organizations as fairer and better for the work-
ingmen than the old system, while the letter carriers are
petitioning for the extension of the civil service law to all
free delivery offices. These two facts show conclusively that

I believe its repeal is no longer among the possibilities, and the great body of the American people are coming to understand and value it. In the recent debate in the House the attempt to cut off the appropriations not only failed, but increased appropriations were carried, which was the greatest victory for the reform that could have been won, and the highest assurance of the permanency of the system that could have been obtained. Public opinion, too, has progressed enormously, as is shown by the fact that even the worst opponents eagerly assert that they believe in real reform, but object only to this particular kind. All this represents a great advance, and is a much greater achievement than most people realize.

What remains to be done? In the first place, it is necessary to demonstrate to the people the practicability and the fairness of the reform methods, for therein rest its maintenance and extension. In the second place, every effort should be made from year to year to obtain appropriations sufficient to enable the commission to carry on their work successfully. In the third place, we must seek the extension of the system by executive act, which can reach almost every branch that it is desirable to bring within the law, and strive also by some practical scheme to take the fourth-class postmasters out of politics. It is utterly impossible to apply to fourth-class postmasters, even if it were desirable,

people generally are more than ready to sustain civil service reform as soon as they understand its practical working, and that opposition to it comes largely from an interested class.

the system of competitive examinations; but it is quite possible to take them out of politics, and to that end every effort now should be directed, for with the removal of the fifty-seven thousand [1] fourth-class post-offices from politics the old system of patronage will be practically at an end. Lastly, and by way of general suggestion to those most ardent in the cause, in judging public men in this matter the same standards should be applied to all, and patronage offices should not be confused with those of the classified service. Do not make haste to criticise, in the hope of partisan gain, the manner in which patronage is distributed, but make every effort to destroy patronage by law; for by law alone can the evil and degrading system of political patronage in the distribution of public offices be rooted out and an American system of fair play and business-like methods put in its place.

[1] There are now over sixty thousand fourth-class postmasters.

THE DISTRIBUTION OF ABILITY IN THE UNITED STATES.[1]

Some time ago there appeared in "The Nine-teenth Century" an article entitled "The Distri-bution of Ability in England." The writer had taken a dictionary of contemporary biography and had classified all the Englishmen therein mentioned according to the occupation in which they had at-tained distinction, and then by the counties in which they were born. In this way he was able to show in what proportion the counties of Eng-land had produced men of distinction and in what department these men had gained eminence. This article suggested to me the idea of writing one of a similar character showing the distribution of ability in the United States by States, and also by race-extraction, which I felt sure would have an even greater interest than the classification made by the English writer, because it was possible here to cover the entire history of a rapidly growing country, and because American States are neces-sarily far more distinct and important social and political divisions than counties could possibly be. I therefore took Appleton's "Encyclopædia of American Biography," in six volumes, one of the largest and most recent works upon the subject,

[1] Reprinted from *The Century*, for September, 1891.

and classified the persons mentioned therein who were citizens of the United States according to occupation, birthplace, and race-extraction.

I began this work, which proved much larger and more laborious than I anticipated, with a feeling of curiosity. But when I had obtained my results I found that they went much farther than the satisfaction of a merely curious inquiry. I am satisfied, and I think any one who will examine dispassionately the tables which follow will be equally satisfied, that the results obtained have a great deal of historical value. The number of names classified and tabulated reaches 14,243, not including the immigrant table, and a number so large includes virtually all the men and women who by their ability have raised themselves even slightly above the general level. The method of classification which I have adopted shows what communities have produced the men who have governed the country and fought its battles, who have educated it and influenced its thought, who have produced its literature, art, and science, and who have made the inventions which in some instances have affected the history of the United States and of mankind.

The classification according to birthplace is as absolutely accurate as is possible in tallying such a large number of names. There are a few instances in which the birthplace was unknown, and these have of necessity been omitted. There are many cases in which the birthplace may be said to have been accidental, and where the person in question had no real connection either by parentage, ancestry, or subsequent career with the State in which he was born. I found it impossible to fix any rule in regard to these cases if I once departed from the actual place of birth as a test. I determined, therefore, to exercise no discretion in the matter, but to credit to each State every one who was born within its borders, no matter whether their parentage and subsequent career connected them with that State or not, and as I am satisfied that these cases in a large degree balance each other I do not think the accuracy of the general result is affected. To this general rule I have made but a single exception. Edgar Allan Poe was born in Boston, but it would have been such a manifest absurdity to credit him to Massachusetts that I have given him to Maryland, to which State he of course really belonged.

While it was possible to be absolutely accurate in regard to the place of birth, and practically so in regard to the occupation or profession, it was not possible to be more than approximately correct on the question of race-extraction. In the first place it was necessary to make the race classification according to the paternal line alone, which is of course partial and, if the French saying that "*les races se feminisent*" be true, is also a misleading arrangement. At the same time, as will be readily seen, it is the only method possible, and moreover the errors arising in this way in large measure balance one another. Taking, therefore, the paternal line as the one to fix race origin, it is

less difficult than might be supposed to determine
what the race origin is. In a large number of
cases, especially where the extraction is not English, the race stock is given in the dictionary. In
a still larger number of instances the name and
the place of birth furnish unmistakable evidence as
to race. That error should be avoided in this classification is not to be expected, but I am perfectly
satisfied that the race distribution is in the main
correct. Such errors as exist tend, I think, here
as elsewhere in these statistics to balance one another, and the net result is, I believe, so substantially accurate as to have very real value, and to
throw a great deal of light on what we owe in the
way of ability to each of the various races which
settled the United States.

The classification which I have described thus
far shows only the quantity, and has no bearing
upon the quality of ability. The arrangement of
the dictionary, however, furnished me with methods
of approximately estimating and distributing ability by quality as well as quantity. A small portrait inserted in the text is given of each person
who attained in the opinion of the editors more
than ordinary distinction, and my examination sat-
isfies me that these portraits have been in the
main so judiciously allotted as to enable us to use
them as a test of quality and as constituting a
class. To the persons having a small portrait I
have given a single star, and in the following
tables there will be found a classification of these
names under that head. A further but much less

valuable classification of the same sort I have given of those to whom were awarded full-page steel engravings. This, I say, is less valuable from the fact that these large portraits do not appear to have been distributed simply on the ground of ability and eminence. For example, an arrangement which gives a place to William Gilmore Simms and shuts out Hawthorne, Poe, and Lowell in the field of literature is manifestly of little weight. In the same way a classification which of necessity includes Tyler, Pierce, and Fillmore, and which omits Jay, Taney, and Chase because they did not happen to be Presidents, is quite misleading as an index of the quality of ability represented. At the same time there is something to be learned from the distribution of these large portraits, especially as their race classification is perfectly accurate, and I have therefore given the persons who have them a double star, and have made a table in which they are classified by State and race.

I have also classified by race and occupation all persons of foreign birth who have gained distinction in this country. I have treated as immigrants all persons who came to the United States after the adoption of the Constitution. It was necessary to draw the line dividing the immigrant from the original settler at some definite point, and for this purpose I took 1789 as the most convenient date. This table, to which I have appended one covering all negroes mentioned in the dictionary is, of course, accurate as to race and birthplace, and will, I think, be found to have an especial value as showing the countries to which we are indebted for ability among our immigrants, and also in what directions that ability has been displayed.

The total number of names classified, apart from the table last described, is, as I have said, 14,243, and these are divided among the States as follows : —

TABLE A.

TOTALS BY STATES.

Massachusetts	2,686
New York	2,605
Pennsylvania	1,827
Connecticut	1,196
Virginia	1,038
Maryland	512
New Hampshire	510
New Jersey	474
Maine	414
South Carolina	398
Ohio	364
Vermont	359
Kentucky	320
North Carolina	300
Rhode Island	291
Georgia	202
Tennessee	136
Delaware	115
Indiana	113
District of Columbia	75
Louisiana	68
Illinois	59
Michigan	44

Amount carried forward . . . 14,106

Amount brought forward . . 14,106

Missouri	39
Alabama	34
Mississippi	26
Florida	12
Wisconsin	12
California	5
Iowa	5
Arkansas	3
Texas	1

14,243

TOTALS BY GROUPS.[1]

New England States	5,456
Massachusetts	2,686
Connecticut	1,196
New Hampshire	510
Maine	414
Vermont	359
Rhode Island	291

5,456

Middle States	5,021
New York	2,605
Pennsylvania	1,827
New Jersey	474
Delaware	115

5,021

[1] I have here, and throughout this article, included in the Middle States New York, Pennsylvania, New Jersey, and Delaware, giving Maryland to the Southern group, to which it properly belongs by settlement, history, population, and, in the main, occupations. For the same reason I have given Kentucky to the Southern, and Missouri to the Western group.

Southern States 3,125
    Virginia 1,038
    Maryland 512
    South Carolina 398
    Kentucky 320
    North Carolina 300
    Georgia 202
    Tennessee 136
    District of Columbia 75
    Louisiana 68
    Alabama 34
    Mississippi 26
    Florida 12
    Arkansas 3
    Texas 1

                                   3,125

Western States 641
    Ohio 364
    Indiana 113
    Illinois 59
    Michigan 44
    Missouri 39
    Wisconsin 12
    California 5
    Iowa 5

                                   641

The foregoing table needs no comment, but the
next, which distributes the totals according to race,
requires, perhaps, a few words of explanation. The
term Scotch-Irish is well understood in this country,
and I have therefore used it, but it is so far from
accurate as an ethnic description that it is almost
a misnomer. The English phrase of " Ulstermen "
is unfortunately no better. The people called

Scotch-Irish in the United States are descendants of the Scotch and English who settled in the North of Ireland, and who made themselves famous by their defense of Londonderry. In some instances there was an infusion of Irish blood, but for the most part these people were of pure Scotch (both lowland and highland) and English stock, and were ardent Protestants. Their heaviest emigration to America began about 1729 and continued with fluctuating numbers until 1774. They have played a great part in the United States, as will be seen by the detailed tables presently to be given.

The Huguenots cover of course the Protestant French who came here during the seventeenth and eighteenth centuries, either direct from France, or by way of England and Holland, where they had first taken refuge. They are quite distinct from those classified simply as French, who are descended as a rule from the original settlers of Louisiana, Missouri, and Illinois, from soldiers who came with Rochambeau, or from refugees who fled here from San Domingo in 1792.

The Welsh enumeration is undoubtedly imperfect. I have included all described as of Welsh origin, and all others where the Welsh extraction was obvious, but there are certainly many Welshmen whom it was impossible to distinguish either by name, or place of birth, and who are therefore counted among the English.

The persons of pure Irish extraction may seem surprisingly few, but as there was virtually no Irish immigration during the colonial period, and indeed none of consequence until the present century was well advanced, no other result could have been looked for.

All the other race divisions are, I feel satisfied, substantially accurate, except, perhaps, for a slight margin of error in each case in favor of the English. It is possible that the Scotch-Irish have benefited at the expense of the Scotch pure and simple, owing to identity of name, but the two classes include virtually all persons of Scotch descent given in the dictionary. The division of the total number by race is as follows:

TABLE B.

TOTALS BY RACE.

English	10,376
Scotch-Irish	1,439
German	659
Huguenot	589
Scotch	436
Dutch	336
Welsh	159
Irish	109
French	85
Scandinavian	31
Spanish	7
Italian	7
Swiss	5
Greek	3
Russian	1
Polish	1
	14,243

The next two tables, C and D, give the state and race divisions, with the distribution in each case according to professions or occupations, showing in what directions the ability of the States and races has been manifested. A few words only are needed to explain the classification. "Statesmen" include not only persons who have held public office, but all who as reformers, agitators, or in any other capacity have distinguished themselves in public affairs. "Clergy" covers not only ordained ministers and missionaries, but all who have been conspicuous in any religious movements, and many of those included under this head, it may be added, have attained distinction in other fields, chiefly as writers. "Literature" covers all who have distinguished themselves as writers, and includes journalists. "Musicians" includes singers, players, and composers. All the other titles are, I think, self-explanatory.

TABLE C.

STATES.	Statesmen.	Soldiers.	Clergy.	Lawyers.	Physicians.	Literature.	Art.	Science.	Educators.	Navy.	Business.	Philanthropy.	Pioneers and Explorers.	Inventors.	Engineers.	Architects.	Musicians.	Actors.	Totals.
Massachusetts	255	246	493	235	167	688	80	131	106	82	118	61	33	43	22	13	33	21	2,696
New York	240	331	364	178	133	568	147	122	82	78	140	51	21	54	54	17	16	54	2,665
Pennsylvania	203	236	306	174	67	297	67	98	76	53	112	10	21	14	12	7	8	22	1,827
Connecticut	147	102	270	127	46	194	33	76	29	31	49	10	34	12	9		8	10	1,287
Virginia	277	234	121	129	40	54	4	19	28	23	49	10	89	14	8		1	8	1,088
Maryland	110	47	84	30	30	55	13	12	9	17	16		9	2	8		2		512
New Hampshire	97	48	63	61	29	35	8	15	29	22	19	4			5		1		519
New Jersey	75	64	65	55	20	34	10	19	24	17	16	5	3	5	4	1		1	474
Maine	106	47	49	39	19	54	7	16	21	11	14	4	2	9	3		2	4	414
South Carolina																			
Ohio	105	91	82	44	35	63	16	21	34	22	14	8	30	11	9	1	4		896
Vermont	62	85	98	41	22	53	15	17	24	5	14	8	50	5	6		2		900
Kentucky	69	71	30	18	19	40	16	14	9	18	14	4	8	7		2	2		729
Georgia	63	82	32	24	12	36	10	15	20	11	19	6	2	1					739
Rhode Island	35	36	20	15	13	18	4	15	7	6	18	3			1				329
North Carolina	64	71	31	37	11	17		14	28	22			4	2	8	1			372
Delaware	32	22	17	18	7	17		11		8	11		3	1	8				201
Tennessee	47	38	21	14	11	16	14	11	8	17		1	2	2	6				195
District of Columbia	23	19	15	12		26	20	14	35	35	11			1	5		3		156
Louisiana	31	22	16	12		19	7	21	23	7			1	1			2		133
Indiana	10	13		12		14	10	14	10	5	16	1			1		1		115
Illinois	5	7	4	8	11			16	14		19		1	2					75
Michigan			3	6	1	14	1	9	6	8	6	1	8						68
Missouri	9	6	1	8	2	6	8	9		9		3	8	1	8			2	59
Alabama	8	9	6	4		9	2	9	6	3	8	4	4		8				44
Mississippi	3	4	3	3		5	1	9	2		3		2		5				34
Florida	8		2	8		9	3	9			6		3	2			3		27
Wisconsin	6	5	1			9			8	2	2		3		1		2		16
California	3				2	9	1	8							8		1	2	12
Iowa		2		2	1	2		3			1	1	2						12
Arkansas	1			1		1		1			1		1		1		3	1	8
Texas.		1		1				1			1								5
																			3
Totals	**2150**	**1892**	**2164**	**1500**	**839**	**2951**	**462**	**564**	**598**	**482**	**559**	**221**	**183**	**169**	**174**	**43**	**82**	**102**	**14,243**

TABLE D.

RACES.	Statesmen.	Soldiers.	Clergy.	Lawyers.	Physicians.	Literature.	Art.	Science.	Educators.	Navy.	Business.	Philanthropy.	Pioneers and Explorers.	Inventors.	Engineers.	Architects.	Musicians.	Actors.	Totals.
English	1542	1299	1639	1100	672	1691	393	441	442	350	402	167	129	136	129	37	62	75	10,376
Scotch-Irish	255	273	221	162	86	131	21	39	64	54	41	14	29	15	14	9	9	13	1,459
German	62	74	165	45	41	90	40	37	18	16	27	8	7	4	16	4	15	8	659
Huguenot	74	95	63	57	37	85	24	22	51	23	33	10	4	5	21	2	4	3	380
Scotch	79	77	80	47	31	47	16	22	16	11	14	6	10	3	7	1	5	4	438
Dutch	56	45	73	40	17	22	6	6	9	11	26	7	2	3	6	2	4	4	396
Welsh	36	25	19	39	12	17	3	6	1	4	4	1	10	4	2		2		159
Irish	9	16	26	12	2	13	2	3		4	4	4	2	2	1			1	109
French	7	14	7	4	4	15	7	3		6	3	2				2	2	3	85
Scandinavian	3		2	1	6	3	3	8	1	1		1	5	2		1			31
Spanish					3	1	1			1			3						7
Italian	1	3			1	2	1	1		1		1		1			1	3	7
Swiss			2						1										5
Greek				1		1		2											3
Russian	1						1		1									1	1
Polish				1		1													1
	2150	1882	2164	1900	839	2051	462	564	596	482	529	221	183	169	174	43	82	102	14,243

TABLE E.

SINGLE STARS — BY STATES.

New York	245
Massachusetts	213
Pennsylvania	113
Connecticut	112
Virginia	94
New Jersey	56
Maryland	50
New Hampshire	35
Maine	34
South Carolina	34
Ohio	32
Kentucky	29
Georgia	25
Vermont	24
North Carolina	20
Rhode Island	20
Delaware	15
Tennessee	11
District of Columbia	9
Illinois	6
Indiana	6
Louisiana	6
Michigan	6
Missouri	1
Florida	1
California	1
Alabama	1
Wisconsin	1
Total	1,200

BY GROUPS.

Massachusetts	213
Maine	34
New Hampshire	35
Vermont	24
Rhode Island	20
Connecticut	112
Six New England States	**438**
New York	245
New Jersey	56
Pennsylvania	113
Delaware	15
Four Middle States	**429**
Maryland	50
Virginia	94
South Carolina	34
Kentucky	29
Georgia	25
North Carolina	20
Tennessee	11
District of Columbia	9
Louisiana	6
Florida	1
Alabama	1
Ten Southern States and District of Columbia .	**280**
Ohio	32
Illinois	6
Indiana	6
Michigan	6
Missouri	1
California	1
Wisconsin	1
Seven Western States	**53**

TABLE F.

SINGLE STARS — BY RACES.

English	856
Scotch-Irish	129
Huguenot	57
Scotch	45
Dutch	39
German	37
Welsh	15
Irish	13
French	6
Scandinavian	1
Spanish	1
Swiss	1
Total	1,200

TABLE G.

DOUBLE STARS — BY STATES.

Virginia	12
Massachusetts	11
New York	7
Pennsylvania	5
Ohio	5
New Hampshire	4
North Carolina	4
South Carolina	2
Connecticut	2
Vermont	1
New Jersey	1
Maine	1
Rhode Island	1
Tennessee	1
Kentucky	1
Total	58

BY GROUPS.

New England 20
Middle States 13
Southern States 18
Western States 7
                                    ———
Total 58

BY PROFESSION AND RACE EXTRACTION.

Virginia . . . . . Welsh . . . . . . 1 Statesman, 1 Soldier,
　　　　　English . . . . . . 6 Statesmen, 2 Soldiers,
　　　　　　　　　　　1 Lawyer,
　　　　　Scotch . . . . . . 1 Soldier 12

Mass . . . . English . . . . . . 5 Statesmen, 4 Writers,
　　　　　　　　　　　1 Inventor, 1 Philanthropist 11

New York . . . English . . . . . . 2 Statesmen, 1 Writer,
　　　　　Dutch . . . . 1 Statesman,
　　　　　Scotch . . . . 1 Statesman, 1 Writer,
　　　　　Irish . . . . 1 Soldier 7

Penn . . . . English . . . . . . 1 Soldier, 1 Naval Officer,
　　　　　Sc. Irish . . . . . 1 Inventor, 1 Statesman,
　　　　　Scotch . . . . . . 1 Soldier 5

Ohio . . . . English . . . . . 3 Statesmen, 2 Soldiers . . 5

N. H . . . . English . . . . . 3 Statesmen,
　　　　　Sc. Irish . . . . . 1 Statesman 4

N. C . . . . English . . . . . . 1 Statesman,
　　　　　Sc. Irish . . . . . 3 Statesmen 4

S. C . . . . English . . . . . . 1 Writer,
　　　　　Sc. Irish . . . . . 1 Statesman 2
                                    ———
Amount carried forward 50

Amount brought forward 50
Conn.. . ... English. . . . . .1 Lawyer, 1 Writer . . . 2
Vermont. . . . .Sc. Irish . . . . .1 Statesman 1
N. J.. . . . . . . .English. . . . . .1 Statesman 1
Maine . . . . . .English. . . . . .1 Writer. 1
R. I.. . . . . . . .English. . . . . .1 Soldier 1
Tenn. . . . . . . .Spanish. . . . . .1 Naval Officer 1
Kentucky. . . . English. . . . . .1 Statesman 1

Total 58

TOTALS BY RACE EXTRACTION.

English 41
Scotch-Irish 8
Scotch 4
Welsh 2
Dutch 1
Spanish 1
Irish 1

TABLE H.

IMMIGRANTS	English	German	Irish	Scotch	Scotch-Irish	French	British Provinces	Scandinavian	Welsh	Belgians	Swiss	Dutch	Poles	Hungarians	Italians	Greek	Russian	Spanish	Portuguese	Totals	Negroes
Statesmen	8	11	13	7	1	2	3	3	1	—	—	—	1	—	—	—	—	—	—	47	14
Soldiers	7	15	19	4	11	7	5	1	1	—	1	1	2	3	—	—	1	—	—	80	1
Clergy	51	72	85	23	30	23	13	2	4	13	4	7	1	2	1	—	1	—	—	337	25
Lawyers	7	3	6	8	7	2	4	—	—	—	—	—	—	—	—	—	—	—	—	37	3
Physicians	15	21	2	10	3	3	2	1	—	—	—	1	1	1	—	—	—	—	—	60	—
Literature	64	30	22	34	12	5	10	3	7	1	1	—	6	4	2	—	—	—	1	201	7
Art	43	22	12	19	1	3	3	2	—	—	3	2	1	1	2	—	—	—	—	112	1
Science	22	16	6	10	—	4	4	—	1	1	—	1	1	—	—	2	—	—	—	75	1
Educators	12	10	7	12	5	7	4	—	—	—	—	—	—	—	2	1	—	—	—	62	5
Navy	2	1	4	—	5	—	3	—	—	—	—	—	—	—	—	—	—	—	—	14	—
Business	16	7	8	13	5	1	4	—	1	—	9	1	—	—	—	—	—	—	—	61	2
Philanthropy	9	1	4	1	10	1	—	—	—	—	—	1	—	—	—	—	—	—	—	19	1
Pioneers and Explorers	2	2	3	1	2	—	1	—	—	—	—	—	—	—	—	—	—	—	—	9	—
Inventors	3	—	—	—	—	1	—	1	—	—	—	—	—	—	—	—	—	—	—	5	—
Engineers	2	9	1	7	1	1	1	—	—	—	—	—	—	—	1	—	—	—	—	23	2
Architects	7	2	—	1	—	1	—	1	—	—	—	—	—	—	—	—	—	—	—	11	—
Musicians	19	20	1	—	1	1	—	—	—	—	—	—	—	—	—	—	—	—	—	46	—
Actors	56	3	7	1	—	1	2	—	1	—	—	—	—	—	2	—	—	—	—	72	—
	345	245	200	151	88	63	60	18	16	15	15	14	13	11	10	3	2	1	1	1271	62

TABLE I.

IMMIGRANTS — SINGLE STARS.

French	Clergy	2
	Actor	1
	Statesman	1
		— 4
Irish	Clergy	6
	Literature	1
	Business	1
	Lawyer	1
	Soldier	1
	Navy	1
		— 11
German	Clergy	2
	Science	1
	Literature	1
	Lawyer	1
	Statesman	1
	Artist	1
	Engineer	1
	Musicians	2
	Soldiers	4
		— 14
English	Clergy	3
	Actors	3
	Literature	2
	Soldiers	2
	Artist	1
	Musician	1
	Philanthropist	1
	Business	1
	Lawyer	1
		— 15
Scotch	Literature	2
	Business	2
	Educator	1
	Clergy	1
	Science	1
		— 7

Swiss	. . . . .	Science .	.	.	.	.	4
		Clergy	.	.	.	.	2
							—6
Scotch-Irish	. . .	Literature	.		.	.	2
		Clergy	.	.	.	.	1
		Business	.	.	.	.	1
		Actor	.	.	.	.	1
		Soldier .	.	.	.	.	1
		Artist	.	.	.	.	1
		Navy	.	.	.	.	1
							—8
W. I. and Prov.	. .	Clergy .	.	.	.	.	1
		Science	.	.	.	.	1
		Engineer	.	.	.	.	1
							—3
Scandinavian	. . .	Engineer	.	.	.	.	1
Belgian .	. . . .	Clergy	.	.	.	.	1
Poles	. . . .	Soldier .	.	.	.	.	1
	Total .	.	.	.	.	.	.	—71

. It is not my intention to analyze the foregoing tables in detail. Indeed, it is not necessary to do so even if space permitted, for the figures tell their own story plainly enough. There are, however, a few general results to which it may be well to call attention. I will take the last table, that relating to immigrants, first. It will be noted that the Irish, who in the general tables contribute a very small number of names, stand third in this table of immigrants, showing in this way that their small numbers in the first table were owing to the fact that they did not come here in the colonial times, and not to any race deficiency. It will be observed, too, in the immigration table that the Irish have contributed more largely to the soldiers than any others, the Germans and Scotch-Irish coming next, and the

English and Scotch being remarkably small in this field. It is also very interesting to note in this connection, especially with regard to some statements that used to be made about the persons of foreign birth in the armies of the United States, that of the men who gained distinction as soldiers, in fighting the battles of the country, 1,892 were native-born, and only 80 were immigrants; while in the navy the disproportion was quite as glaring, 482 being native-born, and only 14 being contributed by immigrants. The largest total amount of ability in the immigration table is shown by the English, and if we add to them the Irish, Scotch, Scotch-Irish, and Welsh, as well as those from the British provinces, we find that the immigration from Great Britain has contributed three-fourths of the ability furnished from outside sources. Germany comes next to England in the total amount of immigrants who have attained distinction, but the largest number in proportion to its immigration is undoubtedly given by France, which furnishes 68 names to the table. Immigration has contributed most largely to the clergy, to literature, and to art, the proportion in the latter case being astonishingly high, 112 immigrants to 147 native-born. On the other hand the immigrants have contributed as little to the statesmanship of the country as they have done to its army and navy.

By the table showing the distribution according to States (Table C) it will be seen, as might be expected, that the oldest communities with the largest white population have been most prolific in

ability of all kinds. At the same time, this rule is
by no means absolute in its application. In Virginia, Massachusetts, and Connecticut the percentage of ability in proportion to the total white population is higher than in the two other leading States,
New York and Pennsylvania. In proportion to its
population, Connecticut leads every other State in
the total amount of ability. In the matter of groups,
not only the absolute amount of ability but the
percentage in proportion to population is higher
in the New England and Middle States than in
those of the South and West outside Maryland and
Virginia.

Even more interesting than the percentages
shown by the totals is the distribution by occupation. There are eighteen departments enumerated
in which distinction has been achieved. New York
leads in eight : soldiers, lawyers, artists, navy, business, engineers, architects, and actors. Massachusetts leads in eight also : clergy, physicians, literature, science, educators, philanthropy, inventors,
and musicians ; while Virginia leads in the remain-
ing two : statesmen and pioneers.

This table also shows that the production of ability has been remarkably concentrated, and has
been confined, on the whole, to comparatively few
States. A few comparisons will prove this. Two
States, Massachusetts and New York, have furnished more than a third of the ability of the
entire country. Three, Massachusetts, New York,
and Pennsylvania, have supplied almost exactly one-
half, and five, Massachusetts, New York, Pennsyl-

vania, Connecticut, and Virginia, have produced
two thirds of the total amount. In the arrangement
by groups, we find that the New England group
and that formed of the four Middle States must
each be credited with more than a third of all the
ability produced. The six New England and the
four Middle States furnish together almost exactly
three quarters of the ability of the country. If Virginia be omitted, it also appears that Massachusetts
alone has furnished a little more and New York
alone a trifle less ability than all the Southern and
Western States together, — that is, than twenty
States and the District of Columbia. In the
Western States the wide difference which exists is
owing, of course, in large measure to their very recent settlement, for which proper allowance must
be made in drawing any deductions from the figures
given in the tables.

Among the new States settled and admitted to
the Union since the adoption of the Constitution,
some interesting results may also be obtained. I
do not include Maine in this division, because
Maine, although a new State, is one of the oldest
settlements. Excluding Maine, then, we find that
Ohio has a long lead over all the other new States,
including Kentucky, which was settled about the
same time, and Louisiana, which was settled many
years before. This striking fact in regard to Ohio
can be due only to the character of the original
settlement.

If we turn now from the distribution by totals
and examine that by professions we find that while

the Southern and Southwestern States, including
Virginia and Maryland, **are** comparatively strong
in statesmen, soldiers, and pioneers, and in a less
degree in lawyers, they are **weak** in all other
classes. The ability of the South, less in **amount**
than that of the New England and Middle States,
was confined to **three or four** departments. In
other words, there **was in** the South but little variety **of** intellectual **activity.** In the Middle States
and New England ability sought every channel **for**
expression, and was displayed in various ways. **All**
the States, in not very widely varying proportions,
produced statesmen, soldiers, lawyers, pioneers, and
clergymen, **and** the seaboard States naval officers.
But almost all the literature, **art,** science, business,
philanthropy, **and** music ; almost all the physicians, educators, **inventors, engineers,** architects,
and actors were produced by the Middle and New
England States. This is a **most** significant fact.
It shows a wide difference between the two civili-
zations, that of the New England **and** Middle
States on the one side and that of the Southern
States on the other ; for the surest tests of civilization in any community are the amount of **ability**
produced and the variety of directions in which that
ability has been displayed. The thirteen original
States were with one or two exceptions settled, and
they **were** all controlled, by men of the same **race-**
stocks and of like traditions. The cause of the
wide difference in amount and **variety of** ability
shown by these tables is a **fresh proof,** if proof were
needed, of the pernicious results of slavery upon even

the finest races.   There never was a more complete
or a worse delusion than the one once so sedu-
lously cultivated, that in this age of the world aristocracy in the best and truest sense and a high
civilization could be compatible with slavery.   No
finer people ever existed than those who settled and
built up our Southern States, but when slavery became, in the course of the world's progress, and in
a free country, nothing less than a hideous anomaly,
it warped the community in which it flourished, limited the range of intellectual activity, dwarfed ability, and retarded terribly the advance of civilization.   It is wonderful that the people who labored
beneath the burden of a slave system achieved as
much as they did, and the mass of ability which
they produced under such adverse conditions is a
striking proof of the strength of the race.   The
effects of slavery are painfully apparent in these
tables, and only time will enable the people who
suffered by the evil system to recover from them.

If we narrow the examination of the tables to
special professions we can get in that direction, also,
many interesting results.   It is possible to point
out only a few of them here.   In literature Massachusetts has a long lead over any other State, and
together with New York and Pennsylvania has furnished more than half of all the writers produced
in the United States.   New York, as might be expected from her large population, is ahead in soldiers and, what was less to be anticipated, in naval
officers also.   Of the total of 1,892 soldiers New
York, Massachusetts, Virginia, and Pennsylvania

furnished the country with 1,047. Ohio, however, in proportion to the total amount of ability, shows among the larger States one of the highest percentages in soldiers, and is far ahead of all those nearest it in total numbers. Virginia leads slightly in statesmen, and with Massachusetts, New York, Pennsylvania, and Connecticut supplies more than half of all produced. New York is far ahead in art, which has come almost wholly from that State and from New England and Pennsylvania. Massachusetts has a similar lead in music, of which New England rather unexpectedly furnishes nearly two thirds. Invention has come chiefly from Massachusetts, New York, and Connecticut, and educators are most numerous in the same group. New York leads in business, Massachusetts in philanthropy, while Virginia is ahead in pioneers and explorers, with Massachusetts a close second.

If we turn now from the table of States to that of races we find that in statesmen and soldiers the Scotch-Irish, Scotch, Huguenots, and Dutch all have a slightly higher percentage in proportion to their totals than the English, while in other directions these four race divisions fall behind the leading race. Other percentages of this kind can readily be made from the tables, but the most interesting question in this direction arises in regard to the proportion of ability to the total numbers of each race. Unluckily, only a rough estimate can be made, for there is absolutely no means of knowing exactly the total amount of immigration in any case. I believe that in proportion to their numbers the Huguenots have produced more and the Germans fewer men of ability than any other races in the United States. I think there can be no doubt as to the Germans, for their immigration was larger than any other in the colonial period except that of the English and possibly of the Scotch-Irish. Their comparatively small numbers in total amounts are emphasized by their further decline in the table of single stars. The explanation is, I think, obvious. The Germans settled chiefly in two or three States, and by retaining their language for at least a century kept themselves more or less separated from the rest of the community. In other words, they did not quickly become Americans. The result was less ability produced and less influence exerted upon the country in proportion to their numbers and natural ability than that of a much less numerous stock like the Huguenots who at once merged themselves in the body of the people and became thoroughgoing Americans. Indeed, if we add the French and the French Huguenots together, we find that the people of French blood exceed absolutely, in the ability produced, all the other races represented except the English and Scotch-Irish, and show a percentage in proportion to their total original immigration much higher than that of any other race. The Dutch suffered slightly, I have no doubt, in the same way and from the same causes as the Germans, while the other immigrants, from Scotland, Ireland, and Wales, did not suffer at all and had no barriers of language to overcome.

The race table, speaking absolutely and not relatively, shows the enormous predominance of the English in the upbuilding of the United States, and if we add to the English the people who came from other parts of Great Britain and from Ireland that predominance becomes overwhelming. The same table shows also what I think is the most important result of the whole inquiry, that the people who have succeeded in the United States and have produced the ability of the country are those who became most quickly and most thoroughly Americans. This is a moral of wide application, and carries a lesson which should never be forgotten, and which, whenever we meet it, should be laid to heart.

NOTE. — This article on the Distribution of Ability has been far more widely noticed and quoted than I had anticipated. It has even attained to the honor of a Japanese translation. It has also excited abundant criticism, and given apparently, in some quarters, much offense. This was not wholly unexpected, for only one race and one State could be first, and there is no pride more sensitive than that of race and locality. I am sorry that I could not arrange the figures to suit everybody's sensibilities, but, unfortunately, it was impossible. I did not create the figures. I merely collected and tabulated them. If, as some of my critics seem to suppose, I had arranged the figures to suit myself, I should not have made Connecticut, among the States, and the French - Huguenots,

among the races, show the highest percentage of
ability. I had no idea what the results would be
when I began, and the statistics are as honest and
accurate as they could be made. The chief objection of the critics whose spirit is moved by local
pride is that Appleton's " Encyclopædia of Biography " was edited by a New Yorker and a New Eng-
lander, and that they favored their own localities.
This criticism seems almost incredible, and yet it
has been made and repeated with all seriousness.
It is easily answered. In the first place, the editors of the " Encyclopædia " could hardly have
prepared that great work with a view to statistics
which no one at that time had suggested. In the
second place, Mr. Wilson and Mr. John Fiske are
incapable of perverting or suppressing historical
material for any purpose. In the third place, a
distinguished American, who does not find a place
in a dictionary of 15,000 names, can hardly have
been very eminent, and accidental omissions of persons who ought to have been included are, as I
know by examination, very few. Lastly, these statistics can be confirmed by others of similar character. Their results are emphasized in proportion
as the list is narrowed to the most highly distinguished persons, as I have shown in a note to the
" Century " for July, 1892.

The race critics are confined to those who think
my figures are unjust to the Irish. I had no prejudice whatever in the matter, and if I had, it
would have made no difference, for I gave the figures exactly as I found them. The pure Irish did

not come to this country in any considerable numbers until nearly the middle of the present century. They therefore show a small total in the
tables based upon race extraction. It could not
have been otherwise, for no race could be expected
to perform the impossible feat of producing ability
in a country where they did not exist except in
very small numbers. In the immigrant table, which
covered the period of their emigration, the Irish, as
I have pointed out in the article, stand very high.

I classified the people from Ireland as Irish and
Scotch-Irish. The latter term is familiar in the
United States, and covers those North of Ireland
Protestants who are chiefly of Scotch and English
origin, who came to this country in large numbers
during the last century, and who rank very high
in the table of race extraction. I believe this classification to be both historically and scientifically
correct. If any one differs with me, he has but to
add the Scotch-Irish and Irish together, and call
them all Irish if he so prefers. But to combine
the two classes, and then accuse me of misrepresen-
tation of the figures because I have divided them
and used avowedly a different classification is, of
course, unfair and absurd. Such criticism, with
much else of a still lower and more ignorant kind
which has been joined with it, is of course not to
be taken seriously, and still less is it worthy of reply.

PARLIAMENTARY OBSTRUCTION IN THE UNITED STATES.[1]

GOVERNMENT by voting and debate through a representative assembly has been peculiarly the work of the English-speaking people. They devised and perfected it, and have carried it from the mother country into all parts of the world. Essentially a governing race, nothing has shown their political capacity more than the success with which they have used this system to secure freedom and to promote civilization. Other nations have since adopted it, and despite many shortcomings it has always managed to live and generally to flourish even in the most alien soil. The theory of government by voting and debate is, first, that the representatives of the people shall legislate and, second, that they shall legislate after debate. If it fails in these purposes it cannot last, for no political system can endure which does not march. In other words, if a legislative body does not legislate, it has no excuse for meeting and no reason for existence, because mere debating societies can be obtained in other and more simple ways, and without expense or weariness to the public.

Of late there has been a growing belief that government by debate is in serious danger of ceasing to march and of doing nothing more than mark

[1] From *The Nineteenth Century* for March, 1891.

time, thus falling into a state of inanition, to the general contempt of mankind. In the December number of "The Nineteenth Century" Mr. Chamberlain, in a very able article, has discussed this danger and the best means of averting it. His article is especially interesting to Americans, because it not only deals with their efforts to overcome existing difficulties in Congress, but shows also in a very pointed fashion that similar difficulties confront the House of Commons. Mr. Chamberlain, speaking with the authority of long experience, makes very clear, what is indeed well known, that in the two great divisions of the English-speaking people, Parliamentary government has come at the same time in both cases to a very critical point, and is in grave peril from abuses of a like nature. This proves, if proof were needed, that these abuses are neither sporadic nor accidental, that they are not due to any particular political question nor to the presence of any given faction or set of men in the representative body. The appearance of similar evils in Parliamentary government both in England and the United States shows that the trouble is neither local nor a matter of chance, but that it is deeply rooted in the system itself, and has been produced by new and changed conditions to which the system must be adapted if it is to continue to work successfully. These new conditions which have produced such grave results are the vastly increased mass of business thrown upon these great governing bodies, and the existence of rules and systems of procedure which are no longer suited to the demands of modern legislation. The evil to which these conditions have given birth is obstruction, as it is commonly called, or more definitely the stopping of legislative movement by a minority of the representatives taking improper but strictly legal advantage of rules and customs originally formed to regulate and facilitate the transaction of business.

In the Congress of the United States the methods used by a minority to prevent action by the majority may be roughly divided into three classes: the refusal of a quorum, dilatory motions, and time-killing debate. From the first of these modes of obstruction Parliament is entirely free, because the small quorum of forty required by the House of Commons makes it practically impossible for the minority to avail themselves of this method of resistance, while the method of voting by division instead of roll-call renders a technical absence by refusing to answer to one's name impossible. In the United States the Constitution fixes the quorum at a majority of the members of the House, thus requiring at the present time the presence of 167 members in order to do business, and it is further provided that on demand of one fifth of the members present the vote shall be taken by yeas and nays. If political parties are at all evenly divided it is almost impossible for the majority party to produce a quorum from its own ranks, and it is always extremely difficult under any circumstances to get an absolutely full attendance of members. The refusal of a quorum has been therefore at once the simplest and most effective method of stopping the passage, or even the consideration, of any measure distasteful to the minority. The practice has been to make some formal motion, the yeas and nays would be ordered, the minority would refuse to vote, and then the point of no quorum would be made and all business would be at a standstill.

When the Republican party came into power in the elections of 1888, they were pledged to such a revision of the rules as would permit the transaction of public business, but they could not even adopt new rules if the minority refused a quorum, for with a majority of only eight votes it was almost impossible to get a quorum of Republicans alone. Speaker Reed met this difficulty by counting those members present and refusing to vote as part of a quorum. The Constitution says that a minority may compel the attendance of members, but says nothing about voting as an evidence of such attendance. Mr. Reed took the ground, commended alike by common sense and by the language of the Constitution, that all the Constitution required in order to form a quorum was attendance, and that members present, whether they voted or not, constituted a quorum. He was sustained in this view that silence and presence constituted acquiescence by the decisions of the courts in regard to corporations and municipal bodies, and by the rulings of many of the state legislatures.[1] The effect of his action was to cripple

---

[1] Since this article was written, the Supreme Court of the United States in a test case has decided unanimously, and in

the most efficient form of obstruction and to make it practically useless, for the refusal of a quorum by actually leaving the House, although it has been attempted, is too violent and difficult to be of much real value. This counting a quorum was the method employed to overcome the worst kind of obstruction or " filibustering " in Congress. It is not necessary to dwell upon it here, because, as I have said, the House of Commons is fortunately free from the difficulties produced by the requirement of a majority quorum.

The second mode of obstruction in Congress has been by means of dilatory motions. The rules of the House in the process of time were gradually developed and elaborated until they became highly technical and were thoroughly understood by only a few of the older members. Formed in theory to facilitate the orderly transaction of business, the rules had not only ceased to serve the end for which they were created, but had grown to be simply a complicated system to prevent legislative action. It would not be profitable, even if space permitted, to enter into a discussion of the various motions which could be used under the rules of the House

a very able opinion, written by Mr. Justice Brewer, that counting a quorum was entirely constitutional. Mr. Reed was fully sustained by the court, and this decision of the highest tribunal in the country settles the constitutional question finally and without appeal. It is now only a question of a very short time when the practice of counting a quorum will be adopted permanently by the House, and in this way we shall be freed from the worst features of this mode of obstruction.

to stop business.   It will suffice to mention as examples the worst and most effective.   Under the
old rules a motion to take a recess and to adjourn
to a certain time, were, like the motion to adjourn,
always in order.   If it was desired to arrest legislative action, a member of the minority would move
to take a recess, or to adjourn, until seven o'clock ;
another would move to amend to half-past seven,
and another would offer an amendment to the amendment to make it eight o'clock.   Thus an indefinite
series of amendments and votes would begin and all
business would cease.   Under the new rules, privilege has been taken from these two motions and
they are no longer made.   There were others less
effective, but of a similar character, which were likewise effaced, and then in addition the Speaker was
given the power to declare any motion dilatory, and
to decline to put it.   These reforms in the rules
brought great and immediate relief, and checked
some of the worst abuses in the way of filibustering.[1]

---

[1] The present house (Fifty-Second Congress), from partisan feeling purely, returned to the old rules, and has suffered accordingly.   But it nevertheless provided that when
the Committee on Rules brought in a rule or order, the
Speaker should have the power to declare any motion dilatory.   This, although limited to a special case, is a full acceptance of Mr. Reed's principle of giving power to the
Speaker to shut off dilatory motion.   Thus the two principles of Mr. Reed's great reform, the counting a quorum
and the refusal to put dilatory motions, have been fully established ; one by the decision of the Supreme Courts, the
other by the acceptance of its opponents.   It is not often that
a far-reaching reform triumphs so soon and so completely.

The last method of obstruction is that which has become unfortunately common in all legislative bodies : the consumption of time by useless debate, engaged in solely to produce delay. The efforts in the House of Representatives to deal with this evil have been going on for many years. What is called closure, or *clôture*, in England and Europe, is known in Congress as the previous question. In the Congress of the Confederation the previous question was the same motion that it still is in the House of Commons. When the new Congress was organized under the Constitution in 1789, it adopted the previous question in its rules, as it had been used in the Congress of the Confederation, and it was not until 1811 that the House decided, on an appeal from the decision of the chair, that the previous question cut off debate, and brought an immediate vote on the main question, thus reversing the original purpose of the motion, and giving to it the effect which it has had ever since. This change gave a majority power to stop debate. In its altered form the previous question has been fiercely assailed as a gag law and as stifling debate, but, nevertheless, without it all legislation would be impossible. It has never been abandoned in America, and nearly all legislative bodies have to-day some motion of similar import.

Stringent as the previous question seems, however, it has had only a partial effect in preventing obstruction. It has never been applied in committee of the whole, and experience has shown that it is there that the most serious delay occurs both in

Parliament and in Congress. Under the rules of the House of Representatives all bills to raise revenue, or which make a charge upon the treasury, but no others, must be considered in committee of the whole. On such bills in committee there is first general debate, for which the time is commonly limited by agreement, and then the bill is read by paragraphs for amendment. During the reading by paragraphs the "five minute rule," which is of long standing in Congress, applies. Under it no one can speak on any single amendment more than five minutes. This rule improves debate, but does not seriously limit it, for amendments, both formal and substantial, can be multiplied indefinitely. Under the old rules the committee was obliged to rise and go back to the House in order to limit debate on a paragraph. Under Mr. Reed's rules this can be done in committee, and the quorum required in committee has been reduced to a hundred, which proved a very wise change. Yet, despite all these limitations, the opportunity for delay in committee of the whole is still almost boundless. Mr. Chamberlain proposes to deal with this evil, if I understand him correctly, by practically abolishing the committee of the whole: a radical reform, indeed, but one which is both wise and necessary, unless the committee of the whole, which is now an almost meaningless survival, is to be allowed to continue with all its temptations and opportunities for fatal obstruction.

Mr. Chamberlain refers in his article to what are known as "special orders," reported from the committee on rules to limit debate, and fix a time for taking a vote on any given measure, as severe contrivances for stopping obstruction. I think Mr. Chamberlain slightly misapprehends the meaning and effect of these special rules or orders. The only peculiar feature about them is, that they give the majority a convenient mode of settling the order of business. Otherwise, they are merely one way of ordering the previous question, or of limiting debate in committee. It really makes no difference in principle, whether the committee in charge of a measure give notice when they call a measure up that, at a given time, the previous question will be moved, or whether the same notice is given by the adoption of a special rule. In either case it is simply the exercise of the power of the majority to close debate, and without the use of this power in some form legislation under modern conditions is well-nigh impossible.

It would be wholly out of place for me to discuss the question of obstruction, or the best means of dealing with it in Parliament. To an outsider it seems as if the opportunities for obstruction in the House of Commons were as yet very imperfectly understood, and as if, despite all that has happened there in that respect, the resources of a factious minority were still largely undeveloped, and would before long demand more effective checks than now exist. It also seems to an American as if the difficulties in Parliament were much less than in Congress, and that whenever they became formidable, there was great readiness in applying a vigorous remedy, **as was done** on sound general principles by Sir Henry Brand **in** 1881, when he took action which appears to us far more arbitrary than any ever indulged in by an American Speaker.

But, whatever **the case** may be as to obstruction in the House of Commons, there can be no doubt **as to the magnitude of the evil in Congress.** In the Fiftieth Congress, elected in 1886, obstruction culminated. It then became apparent to **every one** that, under existing rules and customs, no measure could pass which did not practically have unanimous consent. This is not a fanciful statement. I have seen the House held fast for nearly a week, and **all** movement stopped by the determined action of one energetic man, through the adroit use of dilatory **motions and** points of order. Such a condition **of** things **is a travesty of** representative government. **Where it exists the majority cannot** rule, **while the** minority in the nature of things is unable **to govern. It is, in fact,** the absolute overthrow of majority rule on which popular government rests. Worst of all, it destroys responsibility, for by it the majority is enabled to go to the country, **and to de-**clare that it has done nothing because the minority would not permit it to act. This system was broken down in the Fifty-first Congress by Speaker Reed, supported by the Republican majority. The wholesale waste of time was stopped, although even after **the** reforms it **was** still **wasted** pettily and in detail. **Whether** subsequent Congresses revert to the **old** rules or not, no political party can ever again go before the American people and make the miserable excuse that they have failed to do the public business because the minority would not let them act. Mr. Reed has demonstrated that a majority in Congress can act if it chooses to do so, and no public man has rendered such an important service as this to the people of the United States for many years.

The primary duty of a legislative body is to act. Debate, even when most valuable, is subsidiary. We ought to have always both debate and action, but, if we must choose between them, action must have the preference, for endless debate without action would soon bring any government into contempt. Moreover, the surest way to-day to get intelligent debate is to make it impossible for the minority to stop legislation by obstruction. It has been said that " the business of an opposition is to oppose," and if an opposition can oppose by delay and obstruction they certainly will do so. Take from them this power, and they will then be forced to content themselves with reasonable discussion, which will be of value to the country and the House, and of which they can never be deprived, because enlightened public opinion is sure always to insist upon it. One thing is certain, that, unless parliamentary obstruction can be rigidly restrained, parliamentary government will come into serious peril, for no intelligent people will long bear with a system which is vocal but motionless, which marks time but does not march.

PARLIAMENTARY MINORITIES.[1]

THE question of the rights and position of minorities in representative legislative bodies really involves at the present time the entire subject of modern parliamentary procedure. Yet the extent of the question and its importance are even now but little understood, if we may judge from the criticisms upon the parliamentary struggles of the Fifty-first Congress. Even the nature of the conflict there was the subject of misapprehension. The view universally taken by the Democratic party and its editors appeared to be that not only Mr. Reed's policy, but the problems with which he was trying to deal, were local and sporadic, and owed their existence purely to the lawless efforts of the party in control to get a dangerous and revolutionary power of action. The Democrats and their allies could not see, apparently, that, whatever the merits of the case might be, the question was neither accidental nor temporary.

As a matter of fact and of history, the conflict in the Fifty-first Congress was but one among many which, in varying forms but always with the same principle at stake, had taken or were taking place in almost every country equipped with representative government. We have only to turn to

[1] From the *New York Tribune*, December 26, 1891.

our kin across the sea to find at once a striking
example of the diffusion of this question. The
matter of obstruction by the minority in the House
of Commons and the best way to deal with it have
been for some time subjects of grave discussion in
England, both in the Reviews and in Parliament,
where some very drastic remedies were applied to
overcome it. Yet, in the face of these notorious
facts, one would have supposed, from the outcry
raised here two years ago, that attempts to clear the
way for legislative action were unheard of until
Mr. Reed led the movement for it in the Fifty-first
Congress. That portion of the newspaper press
which calls itself " independent " was particularly
violent on this point, and they and some of their
contributors furnished many fresh and interesting
proofs that educated ignorance, when it exists, is
the densest possible. This is not a paradox, but a
principle. No darkness is so sensible as that which
follows the sudden extinction of a bright light, and
in the same way the ignorance of the educated man
when he steps outside the limits of his education
seems always more impenetrable than any other.

The question of parliamentary obstruction at the
present time is, in truth, almost coextensive with
the existence of parliamentary government. In the
discussion which has arisen over Mr. Reed's rulings, this fact has been pointed out and explained,
but it has received fresh emphasis and most perfect illustration in the last number of " The North
American Review." [1] Nothing that Mr. Reed did

[1] December, 1891.

was received, both in and out of the House, with so
much indignation and surprise as his counting a
quorum.   In the first burst of excitement we were
given to understand that such a thing as counting a
quorum was absolutely unheard of, and the infer-
ence was plainly drawn that such an act was a device
of that personage to whom inventions are sometimes
ascribed, but to whom patents are never issued.
Presently the cries lulled, the first dust subsided,
and then it appeared that, after all, counting a
quorum was not entirely new in this country.   Pre-
cedents, in fact, were found in several State legislatures, and in many municipal bodies.   It was
discovered next that the courts in England and in
the United States, in the case of corporations and
of municipal governments, had held that presence
and silence when a vote was taken constituted
acquiescence.   This was a distinct falling away
from the first idea of complete novelty, but consolation was still found in the theory that, after
all, counting a quorum in a legislative body was
a partisan expedient, the product of American
politics.

To those persons who draw their thoughts and
information from sources outside their own country,
this last idea was very soothing, but even this poor
solace has gone now.   Mr. Theodore Stanton, in the
December number of " The North American Re-
view," has brought together a number of letters
and interviews on the subject of a quorum from
leading statesmen and parliamentarians of Europe.
By these it appears that the doctrine of presence

constituting a quorum is well known in Europe, and that Mr. Reed's position is generally sustained by foreign practice. On the authority of M. Grévy and others of equal repute, we learn that in the French Assembly presence and not the vote is the test of a quorum. The same principle is held in Switzerland. The president of the Belgian chamber says the measure adopted in the United States is practiced in Belgium. In Denmark presence is held to constitute a quorum. Presence and voting are compelled in Norway by heavy fines. The president of the German Reichstag says that a member not responding to his name would undoubtedly be counted if noticed by the functionaries. In Sweden no quorum is required. In Portugal and Great Britain the number required to constitute a quorum is so low that the question does not arise in practice, while in Italy and Holland the question has not arisen at all.

Nothing could show more completely than these facts that, where obstruction takes the form of refusing a quorum, it has been met in other countries in the common-sense way in which Mr. Reed met it.[1] They show also, what indeed needs no additional proof, that, as has already been said, the question of parliamentary obstruction in some form is world-wide at the present time, and that methods of overcoming it have engaged the attention of statesmen everywhere. Instead of its being a nov-

---

[1] Since this was written, Mr. Reed's position as to a quorum has been completely sustained by the unanimous decision of the Supreme Court of the United States. See note, p. 172.

elty, we are rather behind the rest of the world in taking it up. From the appearance, moreover, of the same difficulty in so many countries, it follows that the trouble must be due to general causes, and these causes are so obvious that they do not need very elaborate statement.

The evils of obstruction and the need of their removal are due in the first place to the enormous growth of modern legislative business, and in the second to the increased number of members in parliaments and congresses. When parliamentary bodies were small and the total amount of legislation was not large, it was perfectly possible to deal with everything before the body, and to give each member an opportunity to speak upon all subjects, if he desired, without arresting or even unduly delaying the public business. Rules were framed, therefore, to facilitate the transaction of business under these conditions, but they were not adapted to the new demands, and thus became either hindrances or plainly inadequate when the mass of business was so vastly increased. In Congress, for example, at the present time, only about four per cent. of the business presented is completed. The struggle to be included in that fortunate four per cent. is intense, and the inevitable results are unequaled opportunities and temptations for obstruction in order to either coerce or delay the majority. Under these circumstances it is clear that, if rules are not framed so as to give the majority the power to act, the transaction of the public business even on the most limited scale is at an end. If, for example, unlimited debate is to be allowed, then a minority has an absolute veto on all action. Lungs and language are all that are needed under this system to enable a handful of men to control the legislation of a great nation. It seems hardly necessary to point out the utter absurdity of such a position, and every other abuse of rules and of parliamentary procedure is equally bad.

The theory of parliamentary government and of all government, in the United States, is that the majority shall rule. If the minority has the power to prevent action on the part of the majority the majority no longer rules, and as the minority *ex vi termini* is unable to govern, representative government as we understand it becomes a dismal farce.

The first point, then, in the problem is, as to the rights and the position of minorities. A great deal was said about the rights of minorities at the time of the Fifty-first Congress, and from some of the arguments then advanced one might have inferred that while minorities had rights which might be greater or less, majorities had none. As a matter of fundamental law, the reverse is much nearer the truth. Under the Constitution of the United States the only right actually secured to the minority in Congress is the right to call the yeas and nays and have them recorded. In other words, the Constitution contemplates only government by a majority, and secures to the minority simply the right to make the votes of their opponents a matter of public record. Such other rights as minorities have in

practice are those which have been conferred upon
them by the rules of the House, which are themselves the work of a majority.   In other words,
apart from the single constitutional right of calling
for the yeas and nays, a minority has only the
rights which a majority chooses to give them, and
those rights are the result of custom and public
opinion.   As a matter of justice, of common assent
and of long practice among English-speaking people, a parliamentary minority is entitled to fair play
and to an opportunity for reasonable debate, that
is, to the opportunity to discuss any measure before
the House, and sufficient time to call public attention to it.

It is difficult to see why any minority should be
entitled to more than this: fair recognition in discussion, fair treatment in committees, and reasonable
opportunities for debate.   Yet, on this foundation,
and thanks to the intricate fabric of rules which
had been gradually and unsystematically built up,
minorities in the House of Representatives finally
reached a point where they were able to arrest all
public business, and completely stop action on the
part of the majority.   The evil at last became so
great that a minority of one, by an ingenious use of
the rules, could stop all legislative movement.   It
seems incredible that anybody should have seriously
opposed a movement to break down a system so
wrong and so dangerous as this.   Yet the reform
of the rules of the House, which, in their development and in the presence of the vast growth of
business, had reduced the body to a condition of

legislative inanity, was bitterly resisted at the time, and its scope and meaning are not well understood even now.

It is worth while to restate the simple and fundamental propositions on which that reform rested. The first duty of a legislative body is to legislate. Debate is purely secondary. Our political system has been called government by debate; but if you permit debate to stop legislative action, you have all debate and no government. Debate is highly important, but if either debate or legislation must be sacrificed, the public interest demands that the laws should be enacted even if the talk about them has to stop. There is not, however, the slightest need for extreme measures. All that is necessary is to bring debate within suitable limits, and to do away with obsolete or inefficient rules which serve no purpose but that of obstruction.

The first test of any successful government is that it should march. If a minority of the parliamentary body can prevent all movement, that particular kind of government has ceased to march. The object of Mr. Reed's reform in the House rules was to enable the government to move. The argument is simple, but it seems complete.

Obstruction is, however, not the only evil that has arisen from the overgrown power of the minority. A minority, which is able under the existing rules and conditions of business to stop legislative action by the majority, destroys in so doing responsible government, and no popular government can be safe and sound where official responsibility is lost

or even obscured. In the last few years we have had
a good deal of discussion about responsible government in the United States. It is a good thing to
have our own methods of government discussed
in any way, for the time is not so very far behind
us when the most highly educated people appeared
to think that the institutions and constitutional
government of the United States were hardly
worth serious consideration. In this recent discussion most of the writers belong to the school
which prepares itself by a consideration of English political and constitutional methods, and which,
having formed a standard or a system in this way,
then proceeds to apply it to the United States.

They start with the sound proposition that responsible government is all-important, and that
we need more of it than we have. They then
proceed to find their remedy in schemes to graft
portions of the English system upon ours. This
mode of treatment not only shows a deplorable
lack of originality, but is thoroughly unsound both
historically and scientifically. There is no need
to enter into a comparison of our constitutional
system with that of Great Britain. The end and
object of both is government by the people, but
the methods adopted to reach that end and to carry
on the government are widely different. Whether
our system is better than that of England is not to
the purpose. We think it is; but the point here
is that it is different. Like all stable and successful political systems, that of the United States has
grown gradually, and in conformity with the con-

ditions and the desires of the people. No one questions that improvements can be made. As a matter of fact, our constitutional system has grown and broadened and improved from the beginning. But reforms and improvements must be made in our own way, and in conformity with the laws of our own growth and being.

The suggestion that we should better our system by borrowing something from the English, is the product of the merely imitative mind which is unable to see that such borrowing at this stage is impossible, and would be also both impracticable and undesirable even if it were possible. For example, there are some most excellent people who think that our political salvation is bound up in having cabinet officers or representatives of the executive on the floor of Congress. They utterly fail to see that in order to do that in any way worth doing we must abandon the American system of three coördinate and distinct departments, and place in the hands of Congress in addition to the legislative power the executive power also, to be exercised by a select committee or ministry. It makes no difference whether this is a better system than our own or not. The American people rejected it at the outset, do not believe in it now, and are not going to change the Constitution of the United States in that direction. The immediate inquiry, when this statement of fact is made, is, "Will you, then, do nothing to get a better and clearer responsibility in Congress?" The answer is, "Certainly we would, but that responsibility can be obtained and increased along the lines of our own development, but in no other way."

Another school of writers, of whom the best known are Professor Hart, of Cambridge, and Mr. Lawrence Lowell, have discussed these questions from a different point of view, and have shown that the needed reforms and changes can come, and in due time generally do come, but always in the natural processes of growth, and not by borrowing. This doctrine is not only sound historically, but practically as well. Nevertheless it seems impossible to get it even understood by persons who are unable to imagine any improvements in modes of government in this country except by the adoption of English methods.

Take, for example, the development of the Speakership. The Speakers of the American House of Representatives are constantly being criticised for their exercise of arbitrary power, and nine tenths of this criticism comes from the fact that the minds of those who discuss the question are filled with the conception of the Speaker of the British House of Commons, an officer who differs widely from his prototype on this side of the Atlantic. They do not know what their own Speakership is or has come to be, and they judge it by a standard to which it has no relation. The English Speaker, roughly speaking, is simply a moderator or presiding officer, who lays aside all party ties when he enters on his office, and who has only to perform certain judicial functions in preserving order and carrying forward the business of Parliament. The Speaker

of the American House is all that the English
Speaker is, and is the party chief besides. His
duties as moderator are but a small part of the
work he is chosen to do. He is expected, of
course, to preserve order and decide parliamentary questions; but he is also the leader of his
party, chosen to make up committees who shall
carry out the policy of the party in control. He
is to take a principal part in directing the policy
of his party, and in seeing that the measures agreed
upon by the party are brought to discussion and
decision. In the matter of ordinary recognitions,
of preserving order, and of ruling on technical
points, he is expected to act judicially, and Speakers of all parties have done so. But the American Speaker is also expected, and rightfully expected, to lead his party in the conduct of great
political measures upon which parties are divided,
and, so far as the conduct of the House business
is concerned, he combines the power and the functions of the English Speaker and the English
Prime Minister as well. The development of the
Speakership in this way has brought a personal
responsibility, which, in a body where a Ministry
does not and cannot sit, is of great importance.
Yet the advantage of a clear responsibility which
thus has been gained is generally overlooked, and
the minds of many persons, and of the chief friends
of official responsibility in particular, are absorbed
by a gloomy hostility to the Speaker's great power.

Of all the criticism and discussion upon this
subject, nothing indeed has been more inept than

the talk about the despotism of the Speaker. The
Speaker, in the first place, is the representative,
the voice, and the leader of the majority. They
can create and they destroy. He must carry out
the will of the House, as expressed by its majority,
or he will cease to exist. This state of things is
not in itself the usual underlying condition of a
successful despotism. Then, again, the Speaker's
powers were not exercised, nor even arbitrarily exercised, for the first time in the winter of 1889–90.
They existed before ; they have been growing for
a long time ; and they have been vigorously exerted
by Speakers of all parties.

One example will show better than anything else
the quality and character of the modern Speakership, and dispose of uninformed criticism more
quickly than can be done in any other way. The
greatest power of the Speaker is the power of
recognition. He can bar a member from the floor
throughout a Congress simply by never seeing him.
He can give another member the floor every day
by always seeing him. This vast power is inherent
in the office. No rules created it and no rules can
limit it. Its exercise must remain wholly within
the discretion of the Speaker himself. Mr. Carlisle once used this power in a manner which, in
arbitrary decision, went far beyond any act of his
successor. In the Forty-ninth Congress, near the
close of the session, Mr. Randall, of Pennsylvania,
desired to get the floor to offer a bill relating to
revenue, which he believed would pass by a combination of Republicans and a small minority of

Democrats. The bill was hostile to the declared policy of the majority of the Democrats in the House. The condition of business and the parliamentary situation were such that the bill could only be brought up at a particular time, and everything depended on the Speaker's recognition. Mr. Carlisle refused to recognize Mr. Randall for the purpose of calling up that bill. He took the ground that it was contrary to the policy of the party he represented, and that as the head of that party he would not allow it to come up by a recognition which he was not bound to give by the rules. In all the ordinary business of Congress, both public and private, and on all parliamentary questions, such a position would have been an outrage, and no Speaker would have taken it. But this was one of the great measures of public policy which are few in number, and upon which parties divide. On this Mr. Carlisle took the position openly of the party chief and shut out the bill, as a British Minister would have done. The power and the responsibility went together, and, if he had not done so, his own and his party's responsibility would have been at an end. He took the responsibility and exercised the power, and the official responsibility was thereby concentrated, instead of being lost in a mist of factional combinations.

Mr. Carlisle, in his conception of his position and its power, was correct. He none the less openly took stronger ground and exercised his power more arbitrarily than Mr. Reed, yet he was respectfully treated by his opponents, while Mr.

Reed was made the target of fierce personal abuse
for adhering to the same policy. The difference
was typical of the difference between the parties.
The important point, however, is that the central
and governing principle is the same always. `That
principle is this: Without responsibility, popular
approval or disapproval cannot be had, and there
is no redress for a wrong or support for the right.
With responsibility we have both. If Mr. Carlisle
was acting wrongly the remedy was simple. The
people would take control from him and his party
and give it to Mr. Randall, and then Mr. Randall's
bill would come up. With a biennial return to
the people, the danger of a Speaker's despotism is
not serious, except, perhaps, in the minds of those
who edit partisan comic journals.

Side by side with this development of the Speakership has come that of the Committee on Rules.
The last Congress, when it made a rule giving the
Committee on Rules power to bring in special
orders for the transaction of particular business,
simply formulated what had long been practiced.
In the outcry of the time, the idea was given out
that the Committee on Rules in the Fifty-first Congress were grasping great and unheard-of powers.
As a matter of fact they were only exercising powers which had long been used, but they exercised
them under the definite and legal authority of a
rule instead of that of a mere custom. The power
to bring in special rules and orders is simply the
power to determine the order of business, and it
ought to rest with the majority party. The Speaker

is the head of the Committee on Rules, and with that committee, acting for his party, he has the power to say what measures shall be placed in the four or five per cent. which reach completion. If there is no authority anywhere to select the measures to be passed, legislation in its present crowded state becomes a mere jumble, and nobody is responsible for the failure or success of any measure. Force of circumstances has developed the Committee on Rules into the body which shall select the business to be acted upon, and take the responsibility for that selection, exactly as is done by the English Ministry. This fact has been already pointed out by Professor Hart in a very admirable article. It is a most valuable advance in the direction of getting true responsibility, as it is a native growth along our own lines, but it has met with no favor at the hands of those who care less for official responsibility than for the way in which it is obtained.[1]

But the question of responsibility is much broader and deeper than either the development of the powers of the Speaker or of the Committee on Rules, important as they are. If the minority in a legislative body is to have the power, by any system of rules or through any condition of business, of

---

[1] The present House (Fifty-second Congress), controlled by the Democrats, has still further enlarged the power of the Committee on Rules. It has given the Speaker power, when a rule or special order is reported, to declare any motion dilatory and refuse to entertain it. This is a recognition of the position of the Committee on Rules, and also of Mr. Reed's second great principle, the power of the Speaker to shut out dilatory motions. See note, p. 174.

stopping all legislative action, all political responsibility comes to an end. The majority go to the
country and say the minority would not let them
legislate, and so they are not responsible for what
has been done or left undone ; while the minority,
of course, have merely to say that they were a minority, and therefore, in the nature of things, could
not legislate. To put it in another way, Congress
adjourns, goes to the country, and nobody is responsible for anything. The school of writers to whom
I have already referred like to explain this by saying that it is due to our system of committees, and
because Cabinet officers are not on the floor of the
House. They utterly fail to see that these things
are superficial details, and that the real difficulty
has been that there was no organized body in the
House, either majority or minority, which could be
held responsible for the action of the House as a
whole. The reform, made by the Fifty-first Congress and put in force by Mr. Reed, did something
more important than clear the path for majority
action at the time, great as that service was. Mr.
Reed, and those who sustained him, restored power,
and with power responsibility, to the majority in
the American House of Representatives. For what
was done in that Congress the majority was held
to strict account, and no future majority can ever
go to the people and escape responsibility for their
action or their inaction by saying that the minority
would not permit them to legislate.

Whether the present Congress has rejected the
changes made by Mr. Reed, in whole or in part,

makes absolutely no difference, so far as this point
of party responsibility is concerned. It has been
demonstrated plainly that a majority in the House
of Representatives can legislate if they choose to.
In other words, Mr. Reed and his party, as has been
said, restored responsibility to the majority, and
yet many of the people who have been clamoring
most loudly for the need of increased responsibility
were the first to find fault. This was due partly to
the fact that they did not understand what had
been done, partly to intense party spirit, but, most
of all, to their inability to grasp the idea that
American constitutional development must be along
its own lines, and cannot be advanced by foreign
grafts. Some of them appear to care more for
the shadow than the substance, for the name than
the thing. If they cannot get responsibility in the
English fashion, they seem to prefer that no advance at all should be made. But this narrow criticism and fault-finding does not alter the great fact
that majority responsibility has been clearly established in the House of Representatives, and that the
rights of the minority have been better defined. It
is known now of all men that the minority can no
longer arrest legislation unless the majority chooses
to permit them to do so.

PARTY ALLEGIANCE.[1]

I HAVE been asked to speak to you to-night about political parties, but I do not understand that I am expected to make a party speech. If I were a professional independent I might take advantage of the occasion to urge you to vote for one of our existing parties; but as it is, I shall make a non-political speech, with as little reference as possible to existing parties, or to the political questions of to-day.

It has been the fashion of late years in certain places, of which this neighborhood is one, to decry party organizations, and to take up the attitude that it is a fine thing to condemn all party machinery and organization as inherently bad. My purpose to-night is to consider whether this attitude has any sound justification, either historically or practically, for its existence.

Let us first see how the case stands historically, and as modern parliamentary government conducted through the medium of political parties is peculiarly the work of the English-speaking people, I shall not go outside the history of that people in this branch of the discussion. The first practical

[1] An Address delivered before the students of Harvard University, March 8, 1892.

attempt to carry on party government, as we understand it to-day, was made by a Dutch prince, the
heir of a great name and the fit representative of a
great people. When William of Orange first came
to the English throne he undertook to carry on his
administration by having members of both the
great political parties in his councils. His motives
were the highest, and his desire was to unite Englishmen of all shades of political feeling in support
of the principles and the policies which he believed
to be for the best interests of the country. The result was not satisfactory. In a few years William
found himself with a Parliament broken into factions, and with his policy thwarted by personal jeal-
ousies and temporary coalitions. Under the pressure of circumstances he then called about him men
who all belonged to the Whig party, because, whatever their shortcomings, they were at least united
on the point of sustaining him in the war which
he was waging to curb the power of France, defend
the Protestant religion, and maintain the liberties
of England.

The attempt was entirely successful for the purpose for which it was made, but it was an experiment and an example, rather than the foundation
of a permanent system. Government by parties
did not go on uninterruptedly in England from the
time of William III. The full scope and meaning
of the system, in fact, were not even understood for
many years, and in the succeeding reign government was carried on, at intervals, by combinations
of different groups, who were not necessarily mem-

bers of the same party. Nevertheless, after it had
been once begun by William, the constant tendency
was toward party government, and when Sir Robert
Walpole, one of the greatest Prime Ministers England has ever had, came to his long tenure of power
he gave to the party system a great impetus and
development. Even after his time, however, there
were still relapses to the old practices of combinations between groups and factions, and I think it
may be said that practically it was not until the
time of the younger Pitt that party government,
as we now understand it, was fully established as
a permanent system in England.

In this country we inherited the political habits
of Great Britain, and the party system was so far
developed there when our national government was
founded that it may be fairly said that we have
never known any other. When Washington assumed the Presidency his attitude was not unlike
that of William of Orange. He knew that the
country had just passed through a period of great
and perilous disorder. He regarded the Constitution which had been adopted, and the government
which had been founded under it, as the only means
of making the United States a great and powerful
nation. It seemed to him, with his far-reaching
views, and with the lofty patriotism which always
characterized him, that all right-thinking men ought
to unite in the support of measures designed to establish and confirm the new government. Acting on
this theory he took into his Cabinet men who represented different political opinions and sympathies.

The result was, that party divisions in the United
States began in Washington's Cabinet, and before
his first term was finished he was perfectly satisfied
that he could only carry on his administration successfully by having men of like political opinions
about him. Much as he deplored the perils and
excesses of party spirit, under the severe discipline
of political opposition he became himself a strong
party man.

For more than a hundred years, therefore, the
two great branches of the English-speaking race
have carried on their parliamentary government
by means of political parties. The English Reform Bill of 1832, which was a peaceful revolution, and the maintenance of the Union together
with the abolition of slavery, which brought an
armed revolution, were, politically speaking, the
work of parties. What is true of the greatest
measures is equally true of those of less importance. Therefore it may be said that our history
has been made, and our great advances have been
secured, through party organizations.

Lord Macaulay treats William's experiment at
party government as one of the great achievements of that great man. It may be urged that
Macaulay, writing fifty years ago, did not have
the benefit of those views as to the pernicious
character of parties which have been lately prevalent in certain parts of the United States; but no
such excuse can be made for Mr. John Morley,
who, within a year or two, has given large credit
to Sir Robert Walpole for the work he did in

developing the English party system. We have like testimony from a widely different standpoint. The Duc de Noailles, in a book upon the United States, has lamented that France was without the developed party system, and the same view has been taken by the distinguished publicist, M. Emile de Laveleye. I quote Lord Macaulay and Mr. Morley merely as examples of eminent historians who have considered the party system, with all its defects, — and they are many and serious, — as on the whole a great benefit to the English people, and an essential help to good government. I think it must be admitted that a system which has achieved so much for mankind, which has earned the praise of such high authorities, both English and European, and which convinced William of Orange and George Washington of its necessity in carrying on representative government, cannot be lightly dismissed in deference to anybody's criticism. The question is one that deserves the careful and intelligent consideration of every man who takes an interest, as all men ought to do in this country, in public affairs.

What, then, are the real and solid foundations on which the party system rests? In the first place, there is an inborn division of opinion in human nature itself. Some men are naturally conservative, others progressive. Some men desire to keep things as they are, others insist that they shall change and advance. This is the fundamental distinction which underlies all party divisions. If one side prevailed constantly we should stagnate.

If the other prevailed constantly we should have no stability. It is the collision between these opposing forces which has produced what we call, for lack of better names, human progress and the advance of civilization. These, I say, are the fundamental divisions, but like all things human they are subject to infinite variation. Even in the same man there may be both progressive and conservative tendencies, and this truth is of much wider application in any large group of men. If no broad and general organizations are made in politics, the tendency is for these variations to give birth to an infinite number of groups and factions, each of which agrees within itself on only one thing. The result of such a condition is a constant shifting and changing of men and policies, accompanied by temporary trades, bargains, and coalitions, so that advance is impossible and instability the rule; while at the same time personal feelings hold sway over public principles, examples of which may be seen in France and the South American republics.

Hence it has been found that, in order to secure practical results, it is necessary to combine a great many groups into one large body or party which will agree on certain general principles, and devote itself to putting those principles into action. Thus was originated the political party running, roughly speaking, along the line of division which separates the conservative from the liberal. If you want an illustration in your own history of the practical value of parties, turn to what is known as the era

of good feeling, and learn what their absence im-
plies. When that period arrived, the old parties
formed at the beginning of our government had
settled the issues on which they had originally
divided. All men were merged in one party, or
rather, for the moment, parties in the broad sense
did not exist. The result was, that faction flourished, and there has never been a period in our history when personal politics, which are the meanest
of all politics, were so prevalent, or when public
measures counted for so little and personal ambition and intrigue for so much. English history is
full of like instances, and parties were the natural
resource to which men turned in order that they
might rid themselves of the imbecility of faction.

It was found also, as modern representative government developed, not only that government by
party meant movement as well as stability, but
that it also meant responsibility. Political responsibility is the great safeguard of popular representative government, but in order to have it effective
it must be made simple. No people, in these modern days at least, can go through the long list of
those who are intrusted with their government
and pick out each individual whom they think
should be retained in office. They cannot do this
even with factions. It is necessary to have something that is simpler, broader, and more readily
understood. This simplicity is obtained through
the party system, which concentrates responsibility
upon a single great and accessible organization.

Stability, orderly movement, and responsibility

in political matters are therefore, I think, the foundations and causes of the existence of the party
system in England and the United States. This
system, like free institutions, has not been the
result of accident, but of growth, and the first
question to be asked of those who rail indiscrimi-
nately at the party system is, " With what do you
intend to replace it ? " Its value has been proved
by experience, and the work it does must be done.
If you destroy parties you must have something
ready to fill their place and do their work. Criticism is cheap and plentiful, but I have not yet
seen that essential something in the way of a substitute for parties suggested by it.

Do not understand me as saying that the party
system is perfect. Far from it. Perfection in human affairs, and especially in affairs political, exists
only in the schemes of persons who have never
had any practical experience in dealing with men.
The party system has grave defects, and has caused
serious errors and much wrong - doing. For instance, the responsibility which we get through
parties is of a very rough kind. Many excellent
men are punished because their party is punished,
and many unworthy men prosper because their
party is rewarded. But, admitting all this, it is
none the less true that if you abolish parties, and
allow politics to become a struggle of individuals
and factions, you have no responsibility at all.
Thus it has come about that, in order to get their
political work done in some fashion, the English-
speaking part of mankind, which is fortunately

more concerned with results than with theories, has
formed political parties.

As a rule there are but two, the conservative
and the progressive, the party which marks time
and the party which marches, the party of con-
structive statesmanship and the party which can
only either resist or destroy. The men who com-
pose these two parties, which comprise the great
mass of the people of the country, are both bad and
good, and the party character is that of its average.
Political parties are no more perfect in their com-
position than the party system is in its results.
This is unfortunate, but in the present condition
of man, I fear, inevitable. I have seen a great
many proposals for the foundation of parties to
be composed exclusively of virtuous persons, but
I have never yet met with such a party, small or
large, either in my own small experience or in the
great field of history. The wholly virtuous party
exists thus far, I think, only in the imagination of
persons who have a profound and intimate conviction of their own superiority to the mass of their
fellow-men who are so unlucky as to differ with
them in opinion.

As I understand it, a man supports a party because he believes that on the whole the principles
of that party are right, and that its success in the
long run is for the best interests of his country.
It does not follow that a party man approves of
every party measure, still less that he approves of
all the members of his party. Humanly speaking,
this is a comparative and not an absolute world,

and in political affairs as in many others our object perforce must be to get the best thing attainable. By combination and organization with other men with whom, in a general way, you are in agreement, you can at least obtain some results, when by yourself you would be simply beating your head against the wall and not getting any results at all. This last performance may be an agreeable process to some minds, but it is not of much obvious value to yourself or to humanity.

Such, then, are parties and their purposes as I understand them, and such, also, is the main line of division. It only remains to consider the elements which are ranged outside of parties, and which always include a certain portion of the community. If no man ever changed his politics, and if every one always kept to those he inherited, one party would always be in a majority, and the other always in a minority. In other words, as we know that party power shifts frequently, we are also certain that there is always a body of voters who are ready to change sides. Sometimes a great issue comes along which violently shatters existing parties, and a complete shifting of political power is the consequence. Such changes as these, however, are abnormal and occur but seldom. Parties, as a rule, run along on the great dividing line, and power shifts from one to the other without a political convulsion.

The element which changes the possession of political power under normal conditions is variously composed. In the first place, although politics are largely inherited, there is always a certain number of new voters who make their own choice in voting for the first time, and who thus introduce an element of uncertainty which is invariably present. Then there are the timid people who are afraid of any changes, and are disposed to vote for the party in power, without much regard to what that party is. This is a small and not very important element, but it is felt at times, especially in our great cities.

Finally, there is the independent voter, the man who owns no party allegiance. On this let me be clearly understood. I am speaking now of the real and not of the professional independent. The real independent voter is a man who feels that he performs his highest political duty by voting for one party or the other, according as the success of one party or the other seems to him at the moment for the best interests of the country. He tries both parties by the same standard, be it right or wrong, and he is a good deal influenced by the personality of the candidates. The real independent is essentially solitary and individual, for an " independent party " is a fatuous contradiction in terms. The moment a man enters into combination with other men for political purposes, technically speaking he ceases in so far to be independent, and becomes part of an organization which, to attain a given object, subordinates lesser interests to greater. But the real independent, although solitary in his habits, is one of a numerous class. He does not go to conventions or caucuses or reform clubs, but watches the course of public affairs, and exercises his influence solely by his vote. It has been the fashion lately to talk a great deal about independence in politics, but so far as my observation has gone, the independence in politics of which we have heard so much of late years is the independence of professionals who think the name valuable, and has usually consisted in voting one ticket all the time and in trying the two political parties by widely different standards. Call it by what fair-sounding name you choose, this is partisanship, and unattractive partisanship, because it masquerades. Real independence, using the word in its technical political sense, does not consist in voting any party ticket all the time, nor is its existence proved by vociferation. Independence is a fact and may exist under any conditions, just as the name independence may be claimed and used without any relation to the actual truth. I have seen greater courage and independence shown by men of both parties who were strict party men, and always voted their party ticket, than by any one else, and, at the same time, the most ferocious partisanship I have ever witnessed I have seen exhibited by those who proclaimed their independence most loudly to the ears of a somewhat wearied world.

I said at the outset that when I made a non-political speech, it was not my habit to try to advise or persuade any one to vote for the party to which I belong. But, speaking to you who are just about to enter upon your life work, not merely as men, but as American citizens, I will venture to urge upon your consideration two or three ideas in which

I very profoundly believe, and which are suggested by what I have been saying. Being twenty years out of college is a sufficient misfortune to entitle a man to the privilege of venturing to give advice to his successors here, even at the risk of seeming didactic.

First, then, I would say to you, believe in your country, — be Americans. In the second place, give what you can of your time and thought to your country's service. Give as much as you can, but in any event take an interest in public affairs and do something. I believe you can be most effective in politics by joining a party, that party which by its character and its principles you think can do most for the country. If you are not ready, or if you are so constituted that you cannot become a part of a great organization and subordinate your own wishes to general results, remain an independent in politics. But be a real independent, not a sham one. It is a perfectly honorable thing to be a party man. It is likewise a perfectly honorable thing to be a genuine independent, and to have nothing to do with political organizations of any kind, although I do not think it is so useful. But it is a very mean and dishonest thing to be a party man and call yourself an independent, or to be an independent and call yourself a party man. If you are a member of a party, be true to it. If you are an independent, be true to your independence. But be the slave of neither. Sometimes it is a man's highest duty to separate, either temporarily or finally, from the party to which he is bound by every tie of association and sympathy. Sometimes it is his duty to subordinate himself and his own wishes and preferences to the attainment of some great object, and to go with a party for that end.

Political independence is a valuable thing and a much abused word. To think differently from others, or from a party or a majority, is not necessarily to think independently. Thinking for yourself is the only real independence, and that may lead you into a majority as well as a minority, into a party as well as out of it. It is, after all, largely a matter of seeing things just as they are, and not mistaking names for things. Dr. Johnson, disgusted with the self-styled political "patriots" of his day, defined patriotism as the last refuge of a scoundrel, and in our own time some one has said that, when Dr. Johnson gave that definition, he did not know the infinite possibilities of the word "reform." Both gibes speak the revolt of the healthy human mind against humbug and pretense. Reform is a good, patriotism a noble thing, but those who proclaim themselves most loudly to be their possessors are not necessarily the sole or only proprietors. It is well to be liberal toward other men, for it does not follow because a man differs from you in political opinion that he is therefore less virtuous or less patriotic than yourself. And in this connection let me add that it is well to avoid the superior virtue habit. It is as subtle, as weakening, and as injurious in its way as the alcohol or the morphine habit. A man is most useful who looks upon the world with open eyes, who makes no political fetich of any man, who does not shut his ears to all voices but those which speak the jargon of the parish or the sect, but who strives as best he may to make things better, and to advance enduring principles in such manner as seems to him best, most honest, and most fruitful.

Above all, let me repeat, whether partisan or independent, strive to be just, and to see things as they are. The men who are doing the work of the world are not perfect, and their work is not perfect, but it is under their impulse that the world moves. Take part in the work of the world, and do not fall into the miserable habit of being mere critics of those who are toiling and struggling. Live the life of your time, and take your share in its battles. You will be made thereby not only more effective, but more manly and more generous. You will make mistakes, but, as Mr. Phelps has wisely and wittily said, the man who never makes mistakes never makes anything. It is easy to criticise; it is a much higher and nobler thing to go down into the dust and heat and do something, even if you stumble and fall and rise again begrimed and scarred from the doing. The virtue which is never tested is but a poor virtue, after all.

Let me commend to you the noble words of Milton: "I cannot praise a fugitive and cloistered virtue, unexercised and unbreathed, that never sallies out and sees her adversary, but slinks out of the race where that immortal garland is to be run for,

notwithstanding dust and heat. Assuredly we
bring not innocence into the world, we bring im-
purity much rather ; that which purifies us is trial,
and trial is by what is contrary. The virtue, therefore, which is but a youngling in the contemplation
of evil, and knows not the utmost that vice promises
to her followers, and rejects it, is but a blank virtue, not a pure."

www.ingramcontent.com/pod-product-compliance
Lightning Source LLC
Chambersburg PA
CBHW030124030726

47498CB00007B/2532